D1010578

Connecting Organizational Silos

WILEY & SAS BUSINESS SERIES

The Wiley & SAS Business Series presents books that help senior-level managers with their critical management decisions.

Titles in the Wiley and SAS Business Series include:

Activity-Based Management for Financial Institutions: Driving Bottom-Line Results by Brent Bahnub

Branded! How Retailers Engage Consumers with Social Media and Mobility by Bernie Brennan and Lori Schafer

Business Analytics for Customer Intelligence by Gert Laursen

Business Analytics for Managers: Taking Business Intelligence beyond Reporting by Gert Laursen and Jesper Thorlund

Business Forecasting Deal: Exposing Bad Practices and Providing Practical Solutions, The by Michael Gilliland

Business Intelligence Success Factors: Tools for Aligning Your Business in the Global Economy by Olivia Parr Rud

CIO Best Practices: Enabling Strategic Value with Information Technology, Second Edition by Joe Stenzel

Credit Risk Assessment: The New Lending System for Borrowers, Lenders, and Investors by Clark Abrahams and Mingyuan Zhang

Data Asset: How Smart Companies Govern Their Data for Business Success, The by Tony Fisher

Demand-Driven Forecasting: A Structured Approach to Forecasting by Charles Chase

Enterprise Risk Management: A Methodology for Achieving Strategic Objectives by Gregory Monahan

Executive's Guide to Enterprise Social Media Strategy: How Social Networks Are Radically Transforming Your Business, The by David Thomas and Mike Barlow

Executive's Guide to Solvency II by David Buckham, Jason Wahl, and Stuart Rose

Foreign Currency Financial Reporting from Euros to Yen to Yuan: A Guide to Fundamental Concepts and Practical Applications by Robert Rowan

Manufacturing Best Practices: Optimizing Productivity and Product Quality by Bobby Hull

Mastering Organizational Knowledge Flow: How to Make Knowledge Sharing Work by Frank Leistner

New Know: Innovation Powered, The by Analytics by Thornton May

Performance Management: Integrating Strategy Execution, Methodologies, Risk, and Analytics by Gary Cokins

Social Network Analysis in Telecommunications by Carlos Andre Reis Pinheiro

Statistical Thinking: Improving Business Performance, Second Edition by Roger W. Hoerl and Ronald Snee

Taming the Big Data Tidal Wave: Finding Opportunities in Huge Data Streams with Advanced Analytics by Bill Franks

Value of Business Analytics: Identifying the Path to Profitability, The by Evan Stubbs

Visual Six Sigma: Making Data Analysis Lean by Ian Cox, Marie A Gaudard, Philip J. Ramsey, Mia L. Stephens, and Leo Wright

For more information and a complete list of books in this series, please visit www.wiley.com/go/sas.

Connecting Organizational Silos

Taking Knowledge Flow Management to the Next Level with Social Media

Frank Leistner

John Wiley & Sons, Inc.

Cover image: Michael Rutkowski
Cover design: © Daniel Halvorson/iStockphoto

Published by John Wiley & Sons, Inc., Hoboken, New Jersey.
Published simultaneously in Canada.

Library of Congress Cataloging-in-Publication Data

Leistner, Frank.
Connecting organizational silos : taking knowledge flow management to the next level with social media/Frank Leistner.
p. cm. — (Wiley & SAS business series)
Includes bibliographical references and index.
ISBN 978-1-118-38643-9 (cloth); ISBN 978-1-118-41739-3 (ebk);
ISBN 978-1-118-42193-2 (ebk); ISBN 978-1-118-43444-4 (ebk);
1. Knowledge management. 2. Social media. I. Title.
HD30.2.L4527 2012
658.4′038—dc23

2012026663

Printed in the United States of America

10 9 8 7 6 5 4 3 2 1

To my wife, Inge, and my daughters, Alexandra and Franziska,
your ongoing encouragement and support have fueled my passion

Contents

Foreword xi

Preface xiii

Acknowledgments xxi

Chapter 1 Your Organization Is Not "The Web"....... 1

Terminology and Definitions 1
From Documents to Flows 6
Social Side of Knowledge Flows 7
KFM versus Social Media 10
Case Study 1: The Hub (SAS) 11
Case Study 2: RedNet (Red Ventures) 15
Notes 17

Chapter 2 Why Should You Care about Social Media?....... 19

Motivations 19
Network Dynamics 24
Breaking Isolation 26
The Super Watercooler 29
Handling the Dynamic Organization 32
Innovation Enablement 33
Notes 36

Chapter 3 Getting Started 37

Inside versus Outside Social Media 37

Differences in the World 39

Laying the Foundation 45

How to Really Get It Off the Ground 50

Launch: Project or Initiative? 55

Technology: Build or Buy 56

Notes 58

Chapter 4 Roles 61

More Than Just Socializing 61

Individuals and Departments 68

Mobilize Your Evangelizers 74

Notes 77

Chapter 5 Driving for Success 79

Get All Stakeholders Involved Early 79

Go Viral 82

Freedom within Borders: The Power of Guidelines 85

Training Portfolio 87

Pulse 91

Executive Participation: Not Just Buy-In 93

Notes 96

Chapter 6 Fighting Barriers 97

Fear of Losing Control 97

Unlearning 100

Dealing with "Stupid" 102

Integration 103

No Time to Post: Portfolio Management 110

Legal Concerns 111

Note 114

Chapter 7 Technology: The Enabler 115

Social or Supporting Social 115

I Want an Internal Facebook 118

The Power of Simplicity 120

Multidimensional Navigation 125

Groups or Communities 130

Notification Management 134

Notes 138

Chapter 8 Social Media Analytics 139

Analyze What Is Going On 139

Social Network Analysis versus Reporting 146

Choosing the Right KPIs 151

Notes 155

Chapter 9 What's Next 157

Advances in Technology 157

Dealing with Channel Overload 162

More Social or More Technology 164

Interaction Trends 167

Notes 168

Chapter 10 Final Thoughts 171

Appendix A Key Success Factors 175

Appendix B Additional Resources 181

About the Author 183

Index 185

Foreword

Frank Leistner and I have similar views. We believe that we will create value through the movement of knowledge around our organization in response to a need. The question is how to get this knowledge flow established across the organization, bypassing the various barriers that we encounter.

In the past, we have done this by organizing in the same physical area those activities that work together. This created silos in the organization, each with its own strong culture that developed over time. Today, as we move more and more to a global arena, it becomes necessary to share knowledge across the entire organization. While email is a big step in this direction, it does not allow for the free flow of ideas and knowledge across the organizational silos in a collaborative format, but rather tends to reinforce the existing structure of silos by speeding up communication between them.

To break through the culture of our existing silo structure, and to facilitate new collaborative ventures across the silos, we have found that enterprise social networks (ESNs) are particularly useful. This book is about how to get an ESN established and functioning in your organization on a global basis.

The detail that Frank Leistner goes into by describing all aspects of setting up and managing an ESN is particularly helpful for those of you that are starting out on this transformation of your collaborative framework in your organization.

And, I confess that I learned a lot about how to enhance the performance of such a network even though I have been looking at this issue for many years.

As you try to move along the continuum of knowledge flow, going from communication to collaboration to innovation to speed of innovation in your organization, you will not find a better primer on how to do it than this book.

I recommend it highly.

ROBERT H. BUCKMAN
CEO of Buckman Laboratories, retired, and
Author of *Building a Knowledge-Driven Organization*

Preface

It was April 2011 and the day after I spoke to a group of MBA students, professors, the dean, and some local business representatives at Queens University in Charlotte, North Carolina. I was going to lunch with my friend and host at Queens, Professor Will Sparks. We started reflecting on the night before. It hadn't really been a presentation to be exact—it was more a conversation on stage with questions from Will and the audience.

We had agreed beforehand on a few general topics (mostly from my first book, *Mastering Organizational Knowledge Flow*), but just before we went into the lecture hall to take our seats on stage, I told Will that I was excited to see one of my latest activities, a recently launched internal social network, taking off with great success. During the talk (they call these events "Leadership in Action" at Queens) at about halftime, Will directed the conversation to what I saw as the next stage of knowledge flow management at SAS. And the audience that had been alert all along suddenly became really active, shooting a range of great questions not only about what we had done, what worked, and what presented challenges, but also about social media in general and how to deal with it on a personal level.

At our lunch the next day, Will suddenly said to me: "You should write another book about this. Many organizations are struggling with it, just like they are struggling with getting their knowledge to flow in general."

Since I was still focused on the first book, I wasn't sure I was ready to dive into the next one, but Will had definitely planted a seed in my brain. On my flight from Charlotte to Washington, I pulled out an old meeting agenda and frantically scribbled a few crowded mind maps onto the back. I began to get more and more excited about the idea. I was convinced that there was enough there for another book.

At the time there were a number of social media books out there, and I am sure that while you are reading these lines there is an even greater number of them. However, after looking at some of the titles, I saw that there were a few things that might be unique about the one I had in mind.

The first difference was the link from social media to knowledge flow management—looking at social media within organizations as a key way to enable internal sharing. The success of the first book showed me that there are many individuals who do not care much for complex models and are not satisfied with just an explanation of what the tools are and how they can use them. These readers are looking more for a guide on how they can deal with knowledge sharing through social media on a day-to-day basis. They want to read some real-life, proven examples of what usually works and what does not. They want stories that they can apply on their own journey in introducing social media into their organizations. They want a fairly easy-to-read book that is not too long and has a personal touch to it and provides a balance of day-to-day usable material as well as some inspiring visions. And last but not least, they want a book that is also fun to read.

Those were my key framing ideas while writing this book and I really hope that while you are reading the coming pages, you will discover that I largely succeeded in creating something that brings unique value to you, because that is why I write books in the first place.

Helping to guide knowledge flows in organizations is my passion. When I discovered this discipline (often referred to as knowledge management) in the mid-1990s, I was convinced this would be the right one to fuel that passion.

Over the years, I, personally, have moved away from the term knowledge management (KM) and have come to the conclusion that knowledge flow management (or KFM) is a much better term to use. I also moved beyond the primarily technical view of knowledge as data, and rather consider it to be something that is connected to humans—always. Once it is external of one's mind, it becomes information. If knowledge is what is in people's head, you cannot manage it. What you can manage though is the flow of knowledge between humans.

What is exchanged is information, but as this can be used to re-create knowledge by combining received information with prior knowledge and experience, you can say that in the end it is knowledge that flows.

The biggest problems with the traditional KM view are the focus on technology and the view that a technical construct (like a database) would actually contain knowledge (e.g., the knowledge captured in documents). Document sharing is important since it is one way of laying out information in a way that others can build knowledge from it. But don't be mistaken—a document will never represent the full knowledge that an individual (or group for that matter) might have. It can serve as a great pointer to the one who knows, though.

The issue with documents is that they are fairly costly (in terms of time and effort) to produce, and that situations in today's world are often too complex and fast moving to write everything down. If you observe how people share knowledge these days, you will find that they still like to turn to the person next to them, or call an expert they know. Many times they prefer this to referring to a document, no matter how well it might have been researched and written.

This is where social media comes in. It is another tool and, if you think about it, it is not as new as it might appear. In fact, you could call the watercooler or the coffee machine one of the great social media tools of the last century. The issue with the watercooler and coffee machine is that they do not scale—and scale and high-cardinality, multipoint connection is what the recent social media tools offer, making them very good enablers to support that need for human interaction across distance, when creating a document is too costly or too slow, and it is too hard to get to the right person in time. This does not mean documentation is out of the picture. However, social media extends the portfolio of enabling technologies that make it possible for knowledge to flow within an organization and help to connect silos for better communication and cross-learning.

Social media technology, processes (these are often not spelled out and written down, but rather driven by convention),[1] and related human behaviors are capable of introducing new ways of enablement. As a result, there are new possibilities for collaboration in a more general and multidimensional way (e.g., groups, multiple hashtag dimensions, searches, follower-relations). This means that there are better chances for discovery, faster connection to experts, and faster and wider idea sharing, which all together can drive innovation. Speed is one of the key points. The speed at which dynamic networks can build and the way they can adapt to changing situations is higher than it used to be with tools like mailing lists, document repositories, or even phone lines.

Very similar to other technologies that support knowledge flows, social media needs people to drive and lead an initiative that adds a lot of the other elements beyond the technology. This leadership element is often underestimated. One of the reasons for misjudging the importance lies in the nature of what we often experience on external social media platforms. Facebook, Twitter, and other such platforms seem to have come out of nowhere and grown to hundreds of millions of users. But by the time the majority adopts them, usually a lot of blood, sweat, and programming have gone into their development. As easy as these platforms are to use, to build them was usually not a pure "if-you-build-it-they-will-come" idea. Behind them is usually a single person or small group that had the immense passion and energy to pull it through the bootstrap phase, adjust as necessary, market the idea, and find ways that knowledge about the platform itself could spread in a viral way.

Social media platforms in organizations, also called ESNs, are not self-runners. I am not talking about control and filtering, but rather guidance and strategy to create a flourishing community (or multiple for that matter) that will manage change and flow adaptively—and all this under the guidance of people that have the passion and vision to make it a success.

This book focuses on how social media can lead to success in organizations. The success of social media on the external level has created the increasingly widespread wish for using such technology within the borders of organizations, including but not limited to corporations.[2] The following chapters will not provide exhaustive coverage of all the possible social media tools out there, as there are plenty of books that will introduce you to those. Instead the book will look at the key elements necessary to start an initiative to launch an organizational social media platform and sustain it. As it will outline success factors on the way, it can be equally interesting to those who have already started the process and want to learn about factors that will make their ESN even more successful or save it from future failure.

The audience that will get value from this book is not limited to those in charge of launching and running organizational social media platforms. As more and more organizations deploy these platforms, it is essential that all levels, up to the executives introducing them, equally understand the potential strengths and dangers for the organization. Fear has been a key reason why some organizations have been slower to adopt than others. But fear needs to make way for proper risk assessment, and in order to participate in that phase, executives should not just leave it to their IT or communications department to make all the calls.

Technology is an important part, though, and, especially if you are building your own social media platform in-house, it is essential that those involved with developing or adapting it have a broad understanding beyond the technical features. This book will give them some ideas on how to develop that understanding and have them always keep the human factor in mind to develop a platform that can be successful from a business point of view and not as a technical construct.

Last but not least, the individuals who use the platform as users can gain some valuable insights as well; and by speaking up (and sharing their ideas via the social media platform itself, for example) they can influence success. Individual users are usually at the forefront to provide a lot of the guidance as to what direction a given organizational social media initiative should move. If you, as a user, believe that some useful function or feature is missing, why not speak up and influence others to become part of a movement that will end up in an improvement?

AN OVERVIEW OF THIS BOOK

Chapter 1 sets the stage to position this book, clarify some of the terminology used, and introduce some of the key underlying ideas in broad terms. It will prepare you for the rest of the book. It also quickly outlines a couple of case studies that are used as examples of how you can deal with issues arising during the introduction of an ESN.

Chapter 2 offers reasons why, as an organization or as an individual, you should care about social media. It discusses typical motivations for introducing an ESN and dives deeper into several of the key ways you can provide value to your organization and enhance organizational communication.

Chapter 3 covers topics you need to carefully think about before getting into employing social media tools in general and an ESN specifically. By looking deeper at the differences between what you might be familiar with from external social media platforms and an ESN it helps to lay the foundation for approaching the introduction in a way that sets you up for success.

Chapter 4 names and explains the different roles that individuals will play during the introduction and, equally if not more important, during the life cycle of the ESN. It also provides ideas on when and how to mobilize people to play those roles.

Chapter 5 extends the discussion on success factors beyond the roles to include components like guidelines, training, and the creation of an ongoing initiative pulse.

Chapter 6 provides a slightly different view on the introduction by looking at the main issues with a barrier view. The idea is that knowledge would flow without any issues if there weren't certain barriers from keeping the flow from happening. By looking into the key barriers and offering strategies on how to remove or at least reduce them, you get another set of tools to enable ongoing success for your ESN.

Chapter 7 discusses the role that technology plays in contrast to the social aspects brought to the initiative through the involvement of people. It does not attempt to provide an overview of available social media technologies, but rather introduce some of the key features that an ESN should provide and why those features are essential. Beyond introducing features it also explains processes on how to efficiently use those features.

Chapter 8 talks about ways to analyze and steer the ESN. It offers advice on measuring and reporting and also provides guidance on how to choose proper key performance indicators (KPIs) that you should measure in order to assess and influence the success of your platform.

Chapter 9 offers some outlooks of potential future developments. Predictions in this area are very difficult, as things move extremely quickly. Nevertheless in this chapter I will outline some visions on where organizational social media might move, what technologies will likely be influencing next generations of platforms, and what that might mean for your own initiative.

Chapter 10 finishes with some final thoughts and advice on how to deal with social media for the long term and how to deal with new developments, as outlined in Chapter 9.

At the end of the book, you will find a summary of the key success factors in Appendix A and a few additional reading resources in Appendix B.

I would recommend reading the chapters in order, but if you cannot wait, I am sure you can get value from diving into some of the chapters directly and later use what you learn as a reference should you have issues regarding a given area.

The field of social media is constantly and quickly evolving. New developments in technology will change some perspectives outlined in the chapters you have in front of you. On the other hand, the book outlines some of those principles that I am convinced will hold longer-term, independent of what technology might be used, as well.

Social media is here to stay, as it touches on key principles of human communication. People want to interact with each other. The easier it becomes to interact and the more value people get from doing so, the more likely it will be that they will interact, despite any geographic or organizational boundaries.

NOTES

1. A great example is the convention to use a certain #tag. It is not written down which one to use; someone might start using one and it spreads organically within a community as a term to use to build a connection for a certain topic.
2. For simplicity, I am distinguishing between external and internal here. One recent trend is actually to bridge the two and include external parties by giving them access to (at least some part of) your internal ESN.

Acknowledgments

There are two key elements that need to come together for me to consider writing a book, I have learned. On one side there is the need to have built a sufficient amount of domain knowledge, and on the other side there needs to be a compelling event. In the case of this book, the event was the moment when Queens College Professor Will Sparks insisted on social media platforms in organizations being a topic worth writing about and suggesting to me that I might be a good person to do it. For that spark, I cannot thank Will enough.

What made it easier to enter the book process again was the very positive experience I had with writing *Mastering Organizational Knowledge Flow*. And this is in large part thanks to my editor at SAS, Stacey Hamilton, and all those at Wiley who eased my fears about jumping into such a project. I was very lucky to have Stacey help me, once again, when I was writing the book you are reading now.

Fritz Lehman, VP of Professional Services and my current manager at SAS, was just as supportive as Scott Isaacs, to whom I reported when I first explored the new project.

I am very thankful to all those involved at SAS who have put so much effort into launching our own enterprise social network (ESN) and making it a success. I learned tremendously from them. To start, there is Karen Lee, head of corporate communications and key sponsor for the ESN. With her ongoing enthusiasm she has also made sure that key stakeholders within the organization bought into the concept. My regular discussions with Karen were very inspiring. Becky Graebe and Lainie Hoverstad played central roles in managing the project at SAS and their ideas on how to make it fly were a great inspiration for me. Another great sparring partner was technical lead Joe O'Brien, and his colleague Randy Mullis was a great help in regards to understanding analytical capabilities of the ESN.

A big thank you goes to Wiley development editor Stacey Rivera and all the rest of the staff at Wiley. They do such a great job turning some raw pieces of text and charts into something that looks so much better.

After my last book, I started to increasingly come into contact with other authors and, as they know what is involved in writing, they are always a great inspiration. Just to name a couple that always inspire me with their great positive attitude, I want to thank Michael "MMMMIIIIKKKKEEEE" Raithel from Westat and Chris Hemedinger from SAS, both of them repeat SAS book authors. Chris plays many roles actually, as he is also one of the key activists on the SAS social media front and has been a reviewer of the book as well.

Other reviewers that I want to sincerely thank for their valuable comments are Kirsten Hamstra and Louise Smith. Kirsten has been a key driver of social media for SAS for a number of years, with a central role in coordinating our external efforts. The discussions I had with her over those years have always left me with new ideas. Louise Smith is the SAS Asia Pacific Knowledge Manager and for over a decade she has been a close affiliate when it comes to anything related to knowledge sharing and knowledge flows, apart from being a great friend, of course.

After seeing him on stage at KMWorld 2011, I had a dream candidate for writing a foreword for this book; someone who has reached legendary status in the KM community; despite all his experience, he has stayed so wonderfully young in his thinking. When Bob Buckman agreed to spend the time to read the manuscript and write the foreword I was really honored and proud. A big thanks to Bob. I also really enjoyed the interaction with Barbara McConville, his right hand, who helped to facilitate the process so nicely.

In recent years I have become more and more active within the Swiss KM Forum (SKMF), a great organization facilitating exchanges on knowledge-related topics between practitioners and scholars primarily within Switzerland. Many discussions and some events have helped frame the ideas that I had for the new book. I want to especially thank Veronique Sikora from Business School Lausanne, Gil Regev from EPFL Lausanne, and Pavel Kraus, the president of the SKMF, for their input and ongoing encouragement.

Regular lunch discussions with Beat Meyer from UBS and Beat Knechtli from PwC allowed me to take away some great feedback, new inspiration, and ideas. A big thank you goes to both Beats for listening and offering thoughtful advice.

To get a more balanced perspective on the ideas around social network launches it was very important to have an outside case study to draw from. I want to thank Red Ventures for allowing me to learn from their experiences. It all started with a tour through their incredible facilities outside of Charlotte, North Carolina, in the fall of 2011. A special thank you to Kylie Craig from Red Ventures for spending time on Skype and phone discussions with me to provide valuable feedback on my ideas and views.

Writing takes energy and I want to thank my colleagues at the SAS Switzerland office for energizing me with their interest in the book progress on an ongoing basis: Christine Schieback, Susy Brunner, Barbara Frauenfeld, Leo Gambini, Carmelo Iantosca, Michael Wolf, Karl-Heinz Saxer, Ghislain Wies, and several others have really helped build that energy.

When it comes to providing positive encouragement nobody beats my wife, Inge, though. She knew that the writing phases would steal away time we usually spend together (on weekends or evenings) but nevertheless encouraged me to go for it again. My grown-up daughters Alexandra and Franziska provided their regular thoughtful feedback via Skype from France and Germany as well as during visits in Switzerland. I am very thankful to have such a great family.

Frank Leistner

June 2012

Connecting Organizational Silos

CHAPTER 1

Your Organization Is Not "The Web"

The people who built Silicon Valley were engineers. They learned business, they learned a lot of different things, but they had a real belief that humans, if they worked hard with other creative, smart people, could solve most of humankind's problems. I believe that very much.

Steve Jobs (1955–2011), late Apple CEO, *Wired Magazine*, 1996

TERMINOLOGY AND DEFINITIONS

Most of the terms needed to understand this book are explained alongside discussions of surrounding concepts; however, there are a few terms that are worth spending a bit more time on to make sure there is a common understanding. At the time of this writing, there is a lot of hype surrounding *social media,* and I expect it to be high on the agenda in many organizations for a little while longer. But with so many parties using the term, there is often a range of different understandings and definitions.

Merriam-Webster's Dictionary defines social media as:

> forms of electronic communication (as Web sites for social networking and microblogging) through which users create

> online communities to share information, ideas, personal messages, and other content (as videos).[1]

For the purpose of this book, *organizational social media* should be understood as the collection of tools and processes that support social interaction within any type of private or public organization. Social media tools can come as separate applications (e.g., chat, wikis, social bookmarking, blogs) or in a more integrated networking platform (e.g., Facebook, Twitter, LinkedIn, Tumblr). The term that seems to be catching on when specifically describing networking platforms in organizations is *enterprise social network (ESN)*. Since I will focus on launching those types of platforms, I will use that term accordingly.

A few more words in regards to the term *social*. Why are these new technologies called "social," whereas earlier technologies that also helped people interact (e.g., email, telephone) are not? The difference is in the focus on the lasting social connection. Email lets you interact and engage, but what social media tools and platforms add is a more permanent link between people. A follower relationship on Twitter, a friendship on Facebook, or a connection on LinkedIn, represent more permanent connections that go beyond exchanging information to say, "We have a relationship."

It is also typical for social media relationships to be kept outside of the participants' private spheres. The data as well as the relationship link is not kept in your own playpen but in a system outside of it. Nevertheless everybody owns their data themselves. Today's social networks are different than those that existed in the days of cell phone contact lists because they are actively managed by their participants and can be used to create content and digital cultures. Connections are not built by simply transmitting personal data; they work on a deeper level to include all the defining elements of people as social beings. While people in our network manage their actual social lives, by simply connecting to them we can get very easy access to what is happening in their environment. That makes it quite similar to interacting with friends in real life, where we learn about a wide range of events in their lives by talking with, listening to, and seeing each other. One good example of similar effects in the social media world can be seen on LinkedIn, a business social media network. Users manage simple, individual links between people. These social media connections replace all those business card collections, phone books, email contact lists, and so forth. The beauty of LinkedIn is that a link can stay current even if a person moves from one city, country, or company to another. She simply updates her data in one single place and everyone in her network will have access to her latest phone number, job description, website, email, and mailing address instantly. This resolves the issue of outdated data that existed with managing traditional social networks.

This same principle is also used in syndication methods. You might have heard of RSS feeds, which are basically streams of headlines that use a standard format to syndicate (or disseminate) web content that is frequently updated. RSS was originally an abbreviation for RDF site summary, though it also is commonly called Really Simple Syndication. The simplicity lies in the way that you can leverage content from one place to another on the web.

The word *network* is also used in many different ways, often as a synonym for *web*. Simply put, a network is the infrastructure that power or data moves on. Networking is a verb that we use to describe how we build a collection of connections to other people—people that we have some type of social interaction with. In many cases, social networks are between those with the *potential* to interact, as one person might link to another so that if he ever needed anything from that person in the future he could act on that link. In this definition, social networks are not really new—but the way we can manage those networks across the globe, creating relationships with a single click, is dramatically different and a lot more powerful. Interestingly (and I am not sure if Facebook did this on purpose), the metaphors we use evoke Stone-Age communications; we write on somebody else's wall to leave a message, as prehistoric humans may have done 50,000 years ago when they found a friend's cave empty but did not have time to wait for his return.

In the preface, I talked about the fact that I prefer the term *knowledge flow management (KFM)* over *knowledge management (KM)*, as it more exactly describes what we can and cannot do with it (i.e., manage knowledge that is in people's head). For a complete discussion of the differences between KM and KFM, and how to enable knowledge flow in organizations, I would like to refer you to my earlier book,

Mastering Organizational Knowledge Flow: How to Make Knowledge Sharing Work.[2] (A free download of Chapter 1 is available for on the book's website, masterknowledgeflow.ch.)

As mentioned, I will not go into deep detail on the different social media tools are out there, as you can easily get that somewhere else. But there are a few terms I want to make sure you have a solid understanding of before you read on. One of those more important terms (mentioned briefly in the preface) is a *tag.* A tag is similar to a label that might be used to identify a piece of merchandise. In social media terms, it is basically a word that you use to describe a piece of information. You could also call it *metadata,* as it is data about data. However, tags have taken on an even more central role in some social media platforms, and to understand the power of them in that sense is an important part of understanding the power of social media in general. Good examples of this are the hashtags, which are denoted using the octothorpe (#) and followed by whatever word the user wants to identify.

Users of Twitter, the microblogging service, rely on hashtags extensively. On Twitter, people communicate via messages of 140 characters or less. As part of those 140 characters, users tag certain terms with hashtags to provide more context without taking up space. For instance, someone tweeting about social media could use #socialmedia in a message to indicate that they wish to be part of a larger social discussion about the topic. Once a word or phrase (without spaces) is tagged with the #, it is easy for other users to track, find, and connect with related tweets, posts, links, and content. It also facilitates trend following within a particular network, time period, or community.

The interesting part about tags, and what might seem a little odd at first, is that anyone can make one up. After a while, communities drift toward a common hashtag language, either by explicitly established rules or through a more organic fashion. For instance, when we talked about the juggling convention in Paris this month (yes, I'm also a juggler), participants agreed to use #juglparis2012. On a more organic level, if 90 percent of tweets use the tag #kfm to talk about knowledge flow management, it is a good bet that I will follow suit when I tweet about the topic. It is amazing how quickly this process can happen. People want their tweets to be read and see that others are filtering on certain hashtags, so sometimes a tagging convention will be adopted within minutes. For example, see what happens on Twitter only minutes after some big catastrophe (like an earthquake or tsunami). There might be more than one tag used at first, but very quickly there won't be more than a couple that carry most of the key messages. It is linguistic evolution under a time-lapse camera.

Another way that tags often get pushed is through so-called *tag-clouds*. Tag-clouds are visual tools that show which words are trending in popularity. They are depicted as word collections or clusters where different words appear in different sizes—and sometimes even emphasized using boldface—to show which words are currently generating the most buzz within a particular community. By selecting a word in a tag-cloud, you can view a collection of content in which that particular word has been tagged.

What makes tags so powerful is the way that they can define a virtual context for content without having to draw a fixed link between bits of information themselves. There is no real limit to the number of relationship dimensions being created, and these can change and evolve with extreme speed, especially when compared to fixed taxonomies. I will go more into the power of tags and tagging in later chapters.

For completeness, here are a few more details on blogs and microblogs. *Blog* (short for *weblog*) is a web-based platform that houses content that is created through chunks of text, video, images, and audio that is posted at different time periods. Each entry is usually referred to as a *post*. Blog posts are typically around half a page, but can be longer or shorter as well. The timeline is the key in navigating blogs; usually the latest entry is shown at the top and, as readers scroll down, they can view previous posts. Very old entries are archived away to keep the visible content manageable in size, but they are often accessible through archive browsing and keyword search features.

Twitter is considered a *microblogging* platform, and the shortness of the posts (140 characters or less) means that users create a lot more posts, making the overall platform itself more dynamic. The size limit of tweets is the platform's key feature, and what sets it apart from other social networking sites. While at first one may think it presents a rather large limitation, many Twitter users find that disciplining themselves to stick to 140 characters or less means their posts pack more punch. In addition, users can include a link to an article or blog post that elaborates on a tweet. And to prevent using up too many characters on a single link, one can use a so-called URL shortener (e.g., Bitly, TinyURL, goo.gl) to encode a long URL as a very short one that might not be as readable but will work just as well. URL shorteners are used on many other social media platforms including ESNs, since long URLs may not only eat up valuable characters, but also make text less readable.

FROM DOCUMENTS TO FLOWS

Over the years I have changed my view on knowledge management and arrived at the notion of knowledge flows. I am convinced that *knowledge* is what exists in people's heads, but once it leaves their heads through speech or other content creation, it becomes *information* that needs to be absorbed and integrated with experience to create new knowledge.

This shift was mainly a result of learning from failed KM initiatives that focused primarily on trying to capture knowledge in documents. In those storage models, technology played the central role, but to develop a successful KM strategy, humans must be responsible for that central role. So I widened my view from managing knowledge to managing the flow of knowledge.[3] Knowledge can flow as people exchange information that will be used to create new knowledge at the receiving end (see Exhibit 1.1).

There are a number of other ways that knowledge can flow other than providing information via documents. Good examples include apprenticeships, discussions, stories, videos, and many more. The key is that links are created along which the knowledge can flow, and any barriers that hinder that flow (e.g., missing trust, spatial separation, or insufficient priority for knowledge-sharing activities) be reduced to a minimum.

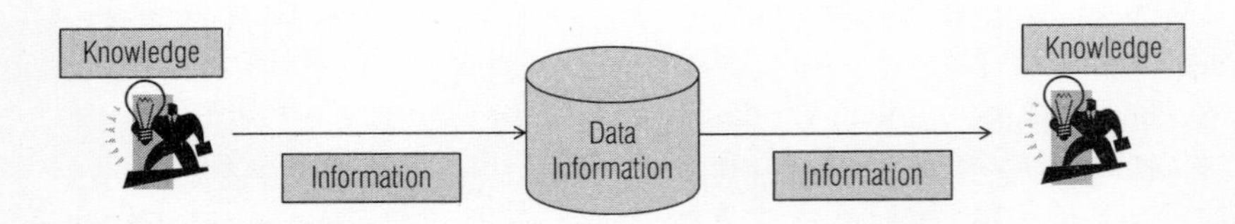

Exhibit 1.1 Knowledge Flow via Information

Documents can still play an important role, but very often in our dynamically changing organizations we do not always have the time or luxury to create full documentation at the same speed that topics and conditions change. In case there is the time to create proper high-quality documentation, it can be the best and most useful way to store and share information. However, it is dangerous to think that organizations can be agile and swift enough to rely on timely documentation alone. As a result, it is worthwhile to explore other ways in which knowledge can flow, and social media falls into that category.

In the last couple of years I have seen a definite trend among knowledge management experts toward using the knowledge flow paradigm.[4] The approach seems to resonate and, when you look at what happens via social media tools, the notion of flow seems to fit very well. It is often undirected, but can be guided, and it can be hindered or blocked by barriers.

SOCIAL SIDE OF KNOWLEDGE FLOWS

One day in February 2011, only a couple of weeks after launching The Hub,[5] the SAS Enterprise Social Network, I was working from home and wanted to do some work via our virtual private network (VPN)—which is the way that we connect from a home computer to the SAS internal network—but when I started the VPN, it failed. The night before I had installed the latest release of the operating system from Apple (OS X) onto my iMac, and I suspected that had changed something.

Luckily, I had also brought my laptop home and that connected to the VPN just fine. But I wanted to resolve the problem, as I often prefer to leave my laptop in the office and use my personal iMac from home. At first I scanned the external web for a solution, but did not find anything about my specific issue. I tried a few tips that I found online, but none of them helped. Next, I sent a help desk request to our internal IT operation. And finally, I posted a question via the status box in my Hub profile, asking if anyone else had installed the new Apple OS X and found a way to get the VPN working again.

Here is what happened: The IT help desk request was routed to the proper person and about three hours later it was being routed to the group that would have a look at it, once its turn came in the queue. (Since my request was not mission critical, I had not set it to the highest priority.) My post on The Hub was answered within 30 minutes, with detailed, easy-to-follow instructions about how the VPN worked under the new version of OS X, and where to download the necessary native VPN files to fix the problem. That by itself was a big value, but what really made this answer special was that on top of the first reply pointing out the solution, there were another two replies from colleagues that confirmed that they had used the described method successfully and quickly.

This interaction demonstrates what social media is all about at its core. Through The Hub I received not only a fast solution, but also confirmation from the community on the value of the answer. This built a high level of trust into the answer. It did not hurt that one of the confirmation comments came from a person I know, but even if I had not known him, the comments would still have had their trust-building effect.

Humans are a social species, which means usually we like to interact. For most people, sharing knowledge within the right, trust-worthy environment is a positive experience. My experience on The Hub was based on stories from people I trusted who had successfully resolved the same problem I was tackling. Stories are an important element for knowledge flows, but in larger organizations, face-to-face interaction is not always possible, so the stories that transport knowledge in a small environment have to be shared differently in a large environment. That is a challenge that once seemed to indicate a key limitation of digital knowledge sharing, but the participative functions of Web 2.0 provided a whole range of ways for people to interact on a daily basis—not only between different sites in the same company, but also across organizations, between individuals, and across major cultural and geographic borders.

Let us look for a moment at how social media has led to flows of knowledge between individuals across the globe that do not know each other. Where did the trust that is necessary for these interactions come from? Part of it is that information exchanges are often very specific and fairly risk-free. For example, if I want to buy a book on the Internet and rely on recommendations from two or three strangers,

I am not taking a big risk. Over time, and by basing judgment on a critical mass of input, trust rises so that those consumer reviews on Amazon are actually of value for my decision.[6] The majority of people commenting on products, hotel rooms, or services intend to share something of value. They are also able to see the value of the collaborative contributions of the crowd unfold.

Another aspect of social media is the important role that teams and communities play in today's work environments. In any type of knowledge work on complex issues, pulling together different minds or splitting tasks into sensible chunks and combining the results in a smart way is essential. Teamwork is not a new concept; but, especially in dispersed, global organizations, teams are increasingly starting to meet virtually. These virtual teams need a portfolio of tools that can help them mimic real face-to-face communication. So far, not many virtual interactions can really compete with face-to-face interactions, but quality is improving. As long as teams combine virtual meetings with regular face-to-face interactions, collaboration will be effective. A quick video discussion transfers a lot more signals than just a phone discussion, for example.

What role can a social media platform play in helping virtual teams? First of all, it can provide a general meeting place that anyone in an organization can usually get to very easily. So, just like anyone else, teams can agree to meet there to create groups (open or private ones) and organize themselves (around topics or projects). But teams usually do not operate in complete isolation either; they have other parties that they interact with to fulfill their tasks. An ESN provides some very good ways to enable this type of connection. The way that conversations are held on an ESN is usually a lot more visible, especially with the history of arguments and counter-arguments. While this history does usually not go back for years, it does document recent discussions very well for all team members to see and learn from. As a result, learning and decision-making are often faster with more participants—either those that are part of the team or others preliminary to the team.

Later in the book, I will discuss the difference between groups in an ESN and communities of practice (CoPs). Just a few words here on teams and CoPs.[7] On the one hand, teams are usually defined entities with a fairly specific membership and project outline. Communities and CoPs, on the other hand, are usually more fluid—members come and go more flexibly and the focus of discussed topics might change over time with the interest of the community members. With this flexibility, communities often benefit from virtual elements, and the potential target member audience could be a lot bigger than that for a normal team.

The flow of membership and topics in a CoP also needs to provide simple ways for people to join and leave based on self-interest and not (as it is often in teams) due to managerial decision to build a certain team. Depending on the topic, it could also be that certain groups that start out as virtual predefined teams exist later as CoPs. All those aspects of dynamic movement are well supported using a social media platform.

Formal documentation is one element of team communication that will continue to have some importance, but at the same time, ad-hoc discussions, question-and-answer exchanges, and highlights of relevant information have always been an important part of face-to-face communication. With the help of social media the more direct engagements are becoming an ongoing available way of interaction that can be used even if team members are in remote locations.

KFM VERSUS SOCIAL MEDIA

In the preface I talked about the importance of knowledge flows and the management of them. So how does knowledge flow management relate to social media?

Social media is basically a collection of tools and the associated processes to use them. Those processes might be outlined and documented, but very often, they are just understood and resemble shared beliefs in the community using the social media tool or platform. One example is the flexible usage of hashtags, which we discussed earlier in this chapter.

Tags do not represent a predefined taxonomy so much as a folksonomy, where anyone can create and spread a new hashtag. You might be able to trace who has used the tag for the first time, but in the end it does not really matter. It matters more who and how many in the community are using it to describe a common context or term.

The ideas of KFM that I outlined in my first book[8] still apply when using technologies like those usually referred to when we talk about social media. But social media itself is not KM or KFM, for that matter. It is a supporting element of reducing barriers that would otherwise hinder the flow of knowledge in an organization.

By providing another distributed network channel, social media tools, if used properly, support better knowledge flows. By making it easy to participate and share, social media empowers a wide range of people in an organization to contribute, including those that might be hesitant to participate in more complicated knowledge-sharing efforts (like contributing to a knowledge base in a more structured way).

As a result, social media tools in general, and an ESN specifically, can reduce the number of barriers that might hinder the flow. Typical barriers that can be reduced are:

- Missing trust
- Lack of connectivity
- Regional and divisional borders (e.g., geographic, based on politics or siloed thinking)
- Awareness of what is going on in diverse communities
- Not-invented-here syndrome (i.e., resisting products and ideas from others)

A successful KFM initiative relies on many aspects that go beyond a social media platform, most of all a supporting and driving team that provides strategy and guidance on an ongoing basis, as well as engaged and motivated users. These do not necessarily come with the technology alone. Similar to other KFM initiatives, one driven by social media will need marketing activities to sell the benefits and make sure a critical mass of users start using the platform in a way that provides ongoing business value to them.

Additionally, users will require some training beyond the technical functionality. Equally important is training on how to use the platform efficiently, whether contributing or using things provided by others.

CASE STUDY 1: THE HUB (SAS)

A number of the lessons and observations laid out in the book are based on a couple of case studies that I was fortunate enough to observe.

For the first, I was closely involved, and able to watch every detail of the process unfold; for the second, I was more remote (geographically and organizationally), but still derived valuable insights from the case.

The first case study is The Hub. The Hub is the ESN that SAS launched in 2011 to support its global staff. It offers the key features that people are used to finding on external social media platforms, including:

- Posting messages and comments to other users' posts.
- Evaluating posts by using a "like" button.
- Following other users to subscribe to their stream of posts.
- Sharing links, photographs, and other documents.
- Creating groups and joining those created by others.
- Providing features in a central environment so that others can follow conversations.
- Creating and using descriptive words (tags) to categorize posts and content on the fly.

In order to give some perspective on the case, I will describe the background and environment this ESN was launched into. SAS, a global leader in business analytics software and services, is a privately held software company that employed approximately 12,000 employees in 53 countries at the time The Hub was launched. It is an organization with a considerable number of technically oriented staff and a large group of developers. In 2011, about 24 percent of revenue was spent on research and development (R&D), and total revenue during that year was $2.725 billion.

Social media and Web 2.0 tools had been in use by employees at SAS since 2005, starting with blogs and wikis, followed by an internal Twitter platform and a social bookmarking site. Upper-management's acceptance of internal employee use of those tools was a process that took time. As in many other organizations, the first reactions, at least by some managers, were cautious. However, it did not take long until some key executives understood the potential and started embracing widespread social media usage.

At the same time, the organization opened up to allow staff to use external platforms like LinkedIn, Facebook, Twitter, and other platforms, as long as there was some business benefit to doing so during business hours. The next step was the formation of committees to look more specifically at how to use those tools for extending engagement with customers and prospects.

Based on some benchmarking and lessons learned from other organizations, the shift to a more active role in using social media started to speed up towards the end of 2008, when SAS hired a full-time social media manager to guide activities. The focus was primarily on guiding employees' activities external to SAS; however, since there is overlap on internal and external usage, the social media manager played a role in guiding purely internal activities as well.

Internally, social media was pushed by a range of groups including the web group, R&D, communications and marketing professionals, and last but not least the knowledge office, including me. Apart from some dedicated drivers, a community of users (most of them also experienced on an external level) started to adopt and evangelize the tools as well.

As a result, a number of social media tools were available and in use within SAS. Not all of them were as widely spread as blogs (currently there are 900, of which 700 are active), but they usually had a fairly good-sized user base across multiple countries. In 2010 it became apparent that certain tools were overlapping in their focus and features, and others lacked some integration. As a result, global communications decided to launch an initiative to look into providing the global SAS user base with an internal social media platform that would integrate some of the most common social media communication tools into one common system. The actual planning was done by a relatively large project team consisting of a wide range of divisions and departments and, as a result, in January 2011 The Hub was launched (see Exhibit 1.2).

Adoption of the new platform was very good, and within a week more than 1,000 SAS employees were using it, which grew into almost 3,000 over the next month. After one year, the adoption rate was greater than 65 percent, and for many it has become one of the key communication tools within SAS. It is used to ask questions and share links, findings, quotes, and tips. It is used during webcasts to ask presenters questions and discuss answers long after the actual presentation is over.

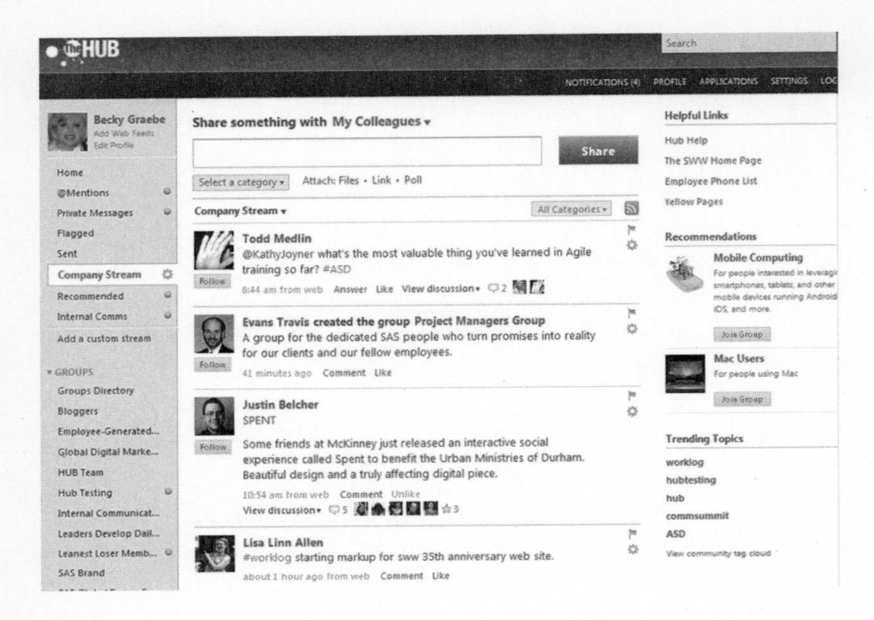

Exhibit 1.2 The Hub at SAS *Source:* © *SAS*

Some events are hosted directly on The Hub like a semiannual innovation day that brings together thousands of staff to share their ideas over a fixed timeframe.

Feedback on the platform over the first year has been very positive. Users are especially impressed by how fast they often get answers to questions, and from the wide range of other employees that they would have never thought about contacting. The divisions that are leading activity are research and development (31 percent), marketing (22 percent), and consulting (12.5 percent), with marketing recently showing the highest growth rates. The individuals in those divisions clearly show cross-communication that did not commonly exist before The Hub. We can already say that collaboration between those organizational entities has increased, which also leads to an even more direct flow of knowledge between the producing, marketing, and implementation arms within the company.

The team that launched The Hub was actually surprised by the widespread adoption, which turned out to be about twice as high as what they had hoped they could reach for the first year.

CASE STUDY 2: REDNET (RED VENTURES)

The second case study concerned a platform that was started at the beginning of 2012. The company that launched it is called Red Ventures and their ESN is called RedNet. Red Ventures is an innovative direct marketing company based in Fort Mill, South Carolina (just outside of Charlotte, North Carolina). When they started the initiative they had about 1,200 employees. The company was founded in 2000 and is therefore a considerably younger company than SAS (founded in 1976).

I learned about Red Venture's plans to launch an ESN in the fall of 2011 during a site visit to their amazing campus and through regular conversations with one of the key drivers of the initiative. I was able to offer some advice and also learn from their experiences launching it.

The initiative was fully supported by the CEO, Ric Elias, who specifically wanted it to be launched to everyone, but in stages. One of the key motivations was to bridge some communication gaps between different campus buildings at their headquarters, but RedNet very quickly offered a lot more than just additional communication channels (see Exhibit 1.3).

One difference in the way the initiative got off the ground at Red Ventures as opposed to SAS was a more careful launch with a pilot group of about 30 users (opposed to the viral spread at SAS). Red Ventures asked 100 people if they would be willing to participate and out of those they selected 30 that represented a good mix for the pilot.

A common element between the SAS and Red Ventures cases was the great excitement of the teams leading the effort (in both cases the effort was sponsored by corporate communications). This positive attitude going into the launch in itself can be seen as a key success factor.

The two companies do have a couple of other things in common, too. They are both known for their employee focus and have been repeatedly acknowledged for their award-winning culture. SAS has been *Fortune* magazine's number-one company to work for in America in 2010 and 2011 (as well as placing in the top 20 several times and also winning similar awards in other countries around the world). Red Ventures won "Charlotte's Best Places to Work for" number-one spot in 2010 and 2011. Agility and speed are high on both companies'

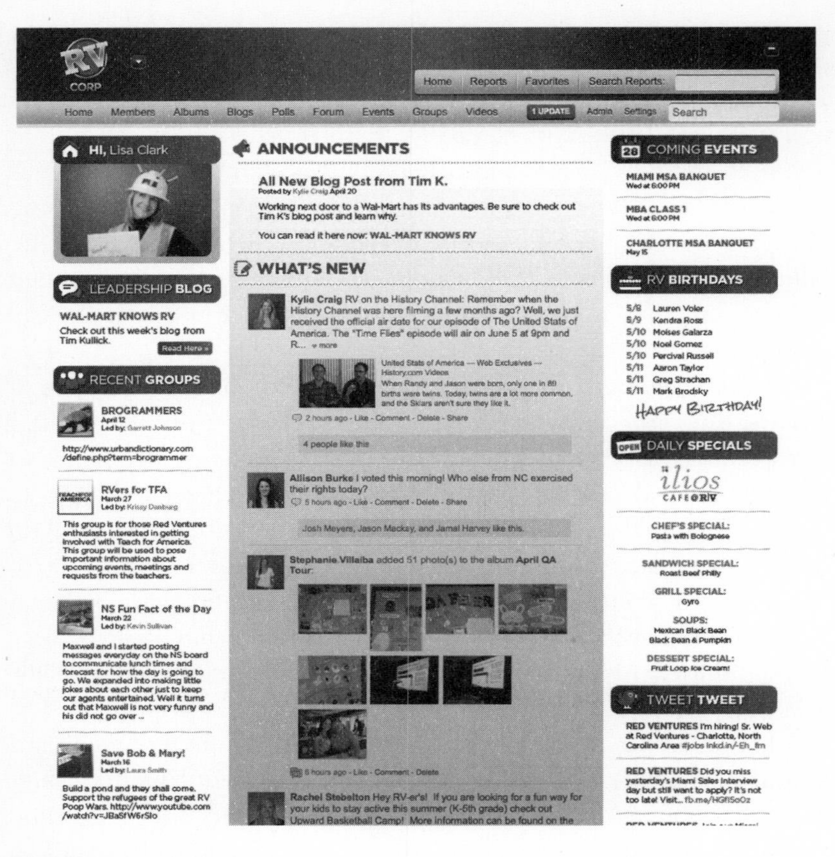

Exhibit 1.3 RedNet at Red Ventures *Source: Copyright 2012, Red Ventures*

radars, and collaboration and communication are drivers for the type of organizations that make it to those top spots.

The question one might ask, of course, is whether the social media efforts succeeded because these companies have a good and open culture, or because activities similar to deploying social media platforms helped build this great culture.

Both aspects likely play a role. In any case, it should not discourage any organization that does not currently have such an acclaimed culture from looking for ways to open up and go that direction. Deploying a social media platform is a lot about trust and trusting employees to do the right things. While it might be more challenging to go there, it might just be one of those initiatives that help improve the culture, if done properly. Why not learn from those organizations that are acknowledged for their culture, and at the same time do exceptionally well business-wise over an extended period of time? Red Ventures and SAS definitely fit into that category.

NOTES

1. *Merriam-Webster's* (online version), "social media." Available at: www.merriam-webster.com/dictionary/social%20media, accessed May 29, 2012.
2. Frank Leistner, *Mastering Organizational Knowledge Flow: How to Make Knowledge Sharing Work* (Hoboken, NJ: John Wiley & Sons, 2010), 183.
3. Ibid., Chapter 1.
4. See Carla O'Dell, presentation from KMWorld 2011 conference, November 2, 2011.
5. For more on "The Hub" see the case study on page 11.
6. It can be debated however if that trust is always justified, as there is a tendency to misuse the system. Websites that use evaluation often try to counter this by adding additional levels like "how useful did you find that comment/rating" or creating a rating of the rater system (like eBay).
7. There are some very good books on the nature of CoPs from Etienne Wenger, one of the fathers of CoPs. Refer to the reading list in Appendix B at the end of the book for more information or just search for Etienne on your favorite book order site.
8. Leistner, *Mastering Organizational Knowledge Flow.*

CHAPTER 2

Why Should You Care about Social Media?

Creativity is just connecting things. When you ask creative people how they did something, they feel a little guilty because they didn't really do it, they just saw something. It seemed obvious to them after a while. That's because they were able to connect experiences they've had and synthesize new things.

Steve Jobs (1955–2011), late Apple CEO

MOTIVATIONS

Why does an organization want to get started with social media internally? There is a whole range of reasons why. Social media is currently getting towards the peak of a hype curve, so one reason to at least look into it is because everybody else seems to be going there. The effects of those tools have been seen on the external web for quite some time and there has been a lot said and written about the potential value—as well as the dangers—of using social media platforms. As a result, an almost natural step is to examine how one could benefit from these tools internally as well.

A first approach in that line of thinking concerns the question "Should I allow members of my organization to be involved in external social media platforms?" The answer to that question very often includes discussions about the potential dangers, as an organization's sensitive internal information might slip out a lot more easily. Consequently, the next stage of thinking concerns the idea of providing a similar tool for internal use, so internal information would actually stay inside the organization's firewall, but still be shared. So the second reason could be framed as offering a safer environment for a social-media–type interaction.

With the growth of social media as a tool to increase awareness of a company, its products, and services comes a need for a better understanding of those tools and processes. People involved in initiatives to run an organization's presence on external social media platforms will have experienced the connection power they provide. From there, it is a short leap to exploring similar possibilities within an organization and increasingly bridging the external and internal worlds with communities that span the firewall. In order to properly manage an external social media presence, it is not enough to limit the target group to a handful of marketing or press people. As many employees are active on platforms like LinkedIn or Facebook, a much larger and more diverse group needs to understand the positives and pitfalls of social media as it relates to their professional lives. An internal ESN can help to get more people trained and familiar with tools and processes within the borders of the organization.

A number of organizations have likely experimented with some individual tools for some time. For example, they might have used wikis for handling collaborative document creation, or maybe they encouraged employees to blog or tweet on an internal platform. Often these initiatives are started by the IT department or, in the case of SAS, the software development groups. Developers are usually very interested in trying out new technology and they have the capabilities to easily create test versions of software platforms. In addition, as a lot of social media tools are open-source, there is not usually a large cost involved that those initiators would have to budget for. Many of these are so simple to use that they take only hours to set up. Often they just build a framework at first and the real application is actually created on the fly as people enter content, links, metadata, and more.

This type of motivation is often based on an individual urge to try out new ideas. As more and more people start using them, these tools suddenly become more widely popular, as they are often easy to use and show—beyond coolness and tech savvy—some advantages over existing technologies. The move to a bigger social media platform often comes when there are multiple tools currently working in isolation and the central IT department has to bring them back together again in order to efficiently manage them. This might happen in stages or in larger chunks.

Apart from these more bottom-up approaches, there are motivations that are driven by current organizational strategies, specifically in regards to communication. They typically are driven by questions like these:

- How can we bridge existing silos in the organization?
- How can we make it more likely that people in the organization collaborate more often and more effectively?
- How can we make sure that people get good and prompt answers to their questions, even if they don't have a clue as to who within the organization might have that answer?
- What can we offer to those digital natives entering the organization that are so used to the Facebook way of communicating with their peers?
- What is the next generation of tools that could help us break knowledge flow barriers?
- How can we cope with the speed of change when documenting everything is just not possible anymore in many cases?
- How can we reduce the risk that people will use external social media platforms to share company information, just because it seems so easy and convenient?

Very often there is more than one reason for introducing an ESN, and bottom-up experimentation might, for example, meet top-down pains and facilitate strategies to overcome those pains.

One reason those motivations are outlined here is to help you gather additional arguments for a business case in your own organization. In addition to those mentioned earlier, it is worth looking at some of the success factors behind why organizations choose to get involved in external social media channels and see how some of those benefits might translate from the extra-organizational world into the intra-organizational world.

A recent study by Harvard Business Review Analytic Services[1] produced a list of benefits that study participants identified. Here are the top eight benefits with a commentary on how this might translate into motivations on an internal organizational level:

1. **Increased awareness of our organization, products, or services among target customers**. Internally, it would be not so much the awareness about the organization, but the awareness of key strategies, new products, and services that employees must keep up with. Especially in larger organizations this can be a major challenge, as information flows on many channels and gets lost.
2. **Increased traffic to website**. Within organizations that already have an established intranet, this will not be as big an issue, but often it is a challenge to lead people to the information that they need. In that case, it is not about just increasing traffic, but making sure the traffic is properly channeled to the sites that bring the best value to those looking for answers.
3. **More favorable perceptions of your organization's products or services.** Brand building is not only an external activity. Just like you are trying to get your customers to like your products or services, it is essential that your employees have a positive perception of them. Through the great capabilities of an ESN to push messages, stories, videos, customer comments, and much more to employees, it becomes easier to build that internal perception and identity as well. One great example from SAS is the way that external customer events are brought closer via The Hub (see Chapter 1 for more information on The Hub) including interviews from analysts and customers with positive feedback.
4. **Ability to monitor what is being said about your organization**. Organizational leaders should be very careful in translating this benefit into a motivation for running an ESN.

For most people, this very quickly translates into the fear of becoming a Big-Brother–like organization. What is important here is not to look at this from an individual level, but rather on a consolidated level. The motivation should be to get a feeling of what some of the big issues are, what the current hot topics are, and so on; not if Joe said something bad about product X. The key to following that road is to keep it away from anything personal. For example, even a tag-cloud that anyone can see has the value of making it more visible what the current buzz in the organization is. On the positive side, an ESN can be a great source for pointers to success stories.

5. **Development of targeted marketing activities.** Usually people think that marketing is done only outside of an organization but, especially when looking at knowledge flow initiatives, I see that marketing is also needed within an organization. Knowledge workers have a choice of how they engage and the old command-and-control methods will not work in those situations. Knowledge workers need to be sold on ideas and motivated to act. An ESN builds a great internal marketing platform by offering a targeted message to a large group of employees via a channel that many in the organization listen to.
6. **Better understanding of customer perceptions of your brand.** This benefit is somewhat linked to item 3 on this list. As much as you can build a brand with an ESN, it is also possible to sense how employees are responding by offering an open forum for shared stories, comments, and discussions that are brand related.
7. **Improved insights about your target market.** If we consider the target market to be a collection of organizational members, an ESN can not only give you some indications about that market by showing key discussion topics, but also a chance to run small surveys to get more specific indicators to key questions.
8. **Identification of positive/negative comments**. While this is definitely a possibility, similar to number 4, this should not be translated into a goal that goes after personal identifiable comments. The danger that comes with analyzing negative comments

on a personal level is that it will kill community trust, which is one of the essential key ingredients you need for a successful ESN.

One important word of caution on the motivations driven by those benefits: The idea is not to misuse an ESN as an internal marketing engine. There is a difference between internal and external marketing activities. On an ESN, word-of-mouth marketing through natural participation in online conversations works, while flooding people on the platform with messages does not. In fact, using it in that way nearly guarantees failure and will kill many of the ESN's benefits. Just like how direct selling on external social media platforms is a good way to lose your followers, the same is equally true within the enterprise. You need to provide value and engage in conversation to influence. People do not want to be hit by commercials from corporate. If you forget this important general social media rule, the ESN will fail quickly.

NETWORK DYNAMICS

Knowledge is a key ingredient of organizational success. In today's knowledge economy this is true for almost any type of organization, whether it is a small startup or a large multinational organization, a high-tech business or a traditional brick-and-mortar setup. Because some of the tools used for enhancing knowledge flows are IT-based, we often think knowledge flow management is a topic for technology companies; but the effective exploitation of the existing knowledge in an organization is a key success factor in any industry and any type of organization, small or large. The basic principles will be very similar, but the methods and tools used might differ. While a very small local organization might primarily use face-to-face interaction to build the network and exchange knowledge, a large, distributed multinational organization will have to employ methods and technologies to bridge space and time.

Such wide distribution is a challenge as much as it is an opportunity. International organizations often have the advantage, for example, to build on a wide range of knowledge, partly influenced by local culture and a wide variety of thinking, which can raise the potential for coming up with truly new thinking and innovation. The challenge is to get knowledge to flow between distributed parts of the organization, as cultural differences, language or dialect, and spatial separation often present barriers that stand in the way of bringing the right ideas together.

The underlying frame for ideas to travel on is some type of network. Even a small local organization with only a handful of people will have some type of network, where certain people are more closely connected with each other than others. People will tend to seek out certain experts for certain needs and answers; a basic example of such a relationship might be a master and an apprentice, who are more likely to interact with one another due to the nature of their positions. But as organizations get larger and more distributed, the question becomes: How can the network develop and flourish for the best use of existing knowledge within the organization. The interesting part about networks is that they are nonlinear constructs. With more and more nodes in the network (people), the number of links (relationships) grows dramatically. A relationship within a social network is created, for example, by following another person. Following indicates that a user would like to be updated on another user's posts, often by having them show up in their home stream of messages. Reciprocity is not mandatory, so if someone follows me, I don't need to follow him back. But it happens relatively often that people do choose to follow their own followers, especially when they share topical interests. An exception to this is executives. Many employees follow their company's top-level executives to stay current on company news and statements, but it is unlikely that executives will reciprocate all of those links.

While the follower relationship is one of the most obvious ways people connect, relationships are also built in social media platforms by joining groups and watching ongoing posts, discussions, and comments.

Here is an example as to the degree that those relationships can grow: When SAS reached about 8,000 registered users on The Hub, the total number of follows had reached 360,000. Those links present a large potential of information and idea flow. Of course the existence of the link does not guarantee any value. Especially if not properly managed, connections can become a source of spam, distraction, and, eventually, information overload.

As we see from the dramatic connectivity growth on the Internet, which puts information from almost anywhere on the planet at our fingertips, the opportunity this provides businesses and individuals is huge. In the case of an organization, it would be dangerous not to take advantage of digital connectivity strategically and managing the potential downsides to maximize value.

BREAKING ISOLATION

If you needed to describe in one single word what social media platforms offer, the best one in my mind is proximity. Traditional social networks (i.e., those in the real, nondigital world) are usually limited to meetings at regular intervals. In the Stone Age, people interacted only locally and when they physically saw each other. With more and faster ways to travel and communicate, it became easier to create the proximity for building network ties.

The Hanseatic League was a famous trade organization that existed from the 12th to the 17th century and connected a number of cities in northern Europe. Networking was a very important part of the business, but in-person meetings happened on a monthly basis, at best, depending on where people were located. With today's ease of travel via plane, networking on a global level has become a lot easier, but it still takes a day travel from the United States to Australia, meaning the costs (in every sense) for such interactions are considerable. Face-to-face contact offers a number of different channels that cannot be replaced by virtual interaction, even today, but with audio and video we are getting closer. In fact, gestures, smell, ambiance, and much more cannot be underestimated, as communication is up to 80 percent nonverbal.

Nevertheless, frequent interaction through a social media platform can make up for some of it and enrich face-to-face meetings when they happen. Through exchanging stories and getting more familiar with each other online, the trust element is increased—an important component for effective communication and knowledge sharing. We have found in our ESN at SAS that certain employees that used to be more isolated in their work, suddenly get more connected. We heard that feedback several times from those working in home offices. By connecting to others on a nonwork social level about something they are really passionate about (e.g., cars, soccer, or photography), they feel more connected to others and the organization.

A 2012 study by Gagen MacDonald[2] found that 61 percent of employees find it easier to collaborate with others using an ESN. When something is easier, people do it more often and consequently they feel more connected. Another study, published in 2011 by McKinsey,[3] found that 51 percent of employees saw an increase in the speed of accessing internal experts and 74 percent saw an increase in the speed of accessing knowledge in general after ESN implementation. What was interesting about that study was that those percentages went down slightly from 2010, which showed numbers of 52 percent and 77 percent, respectively. This could be the first sign of a flattening hype curve, but I expect those benefits to stabilize over time.

Engagement with others works to reduce isolation on a personal level as well as on a technical level. People get more input, learn more, and feel more positive about themselves as a result. Especially the connection to other experts within the organization can help build ties that not only lead to personal benefits, but also to more efficiency and silo-bridging for the organization as a whole.

In general, isolation also diminishes conversation. If you have a larger number of employees working at one site, they will engage in conversations frequently (e.g., in the elevator, in the coffee room, at the watercooler, during lunch, and of course in any type of business situation). However, it is the combination of those that are planned and those spontaneous that provides valuable inputs, spawns ideas, and creates a common sense of belonging. Missing out on the majority of those conversations can lead to disengagement and isolation, an effect that home-office workers have to spend quite an effort to fight against—and some do better than others in this discipline.

An additional factor that can occur is the isolation of people from the knowledge that they need. This can occur, for example, when people enter or leave an organization or move around within it. (Later in this chapter we will discuss dynamic organizations.)

On-boarding is the process in which those entering an organization acquire knowledge as quickly as possible to be able to handle the new job they are asked to perform. A proper hand-over, as much as it would be great to have, is not always easy. The person formerly in that role might have left already, the people that are supposed to share the relevant knowledge to get started might be too busy, or the right knowledge might not be available, especially if it is a job with a newly developed profile.

The wider community provided by an ESN can be just the place where people can ask diverse questions about elements of their new job. It might actually be easier to ask an ESN community rather than track down the information in some other way. After a relatively short time, many new hires feel they are expected to know something and may be too embarrassed to ask questions, especially about something they have asked for help with before. An ESN community is used to dealing with newcomers and is less likely to judge a question as being foolish or something that the employee should already understand. Also, the benefit of scale comes into play. While on a local level you might have a couple of people that can help you, on a global ESN you probably have many more. This approach could also result in getting new answers to old questions, which means even though you are a newcomer you might quickly become a source of information for the rest of the social network and your immediate colleagues.

One additional effect that we have seen repeatedly with The Hub is the warm welcome of new employees. By identifying herself as being new to the organization, a new employee's question is framed in context. Quite often new hires not only receive answers to their questions, but also get additional words of hearty welcome, support, and more general advice that will help new employees get started faster. In some cases those replies include pointers to additional introductory resources. Recently on The Hub, a new group was founded specifically for new employees to highlight the locations of useful and available resources.

The other end of the employee life cycle is leaving the organization. One of the biggest reasons why people might want to turn to knowledge management (KM) in general is to combat knowledge loss when people depart. One approach is to try to capture as much information as possible during ongoing processes so if a key person leaves, the knowledge remains. However, what is captured through this process is still information, which will need interpretation and understanding by people to become new knowledge.

This approach often captures only a few of the total number of dimensions of knowledge that an expert might have. Another approach is transferring that knowledge on an ongoing basis. Communities of practice (CoPs) are a great way of sharing knowledge, spreading it, and embedding it into a larger part of the organization, such that the departure of a single member of the community will not have as dramatic an effect. An ESN can be a great platform to keep conversations happening within communities and across them as well. This increases the spreading and embedding of knowledge immediately. If you keep the conversations for an extended time, you can also make them searchable. While longer-term storage is always seen as a key KM benefit, I would be careful with your expectations of this in larger organizations.

An ESN is primarily a conversation engine and not another document repository. To keep the conversation fresh and not overload users with old content, SAS is archiving the content after half a year, as long as it is not active anymore (comments restart the counter). Employees are asked to move longer-term valuable content into other repositories or create longer documents outside (e.g., in a blog) in the first place and just point to it via The Hub.

Keep in mind that conversations themselves do not always provide value; sometimes they merely offer the potential to lead to valuable exchanges and support the creation of new knowledge. In order for conversations to have value on their own, they have to have substance as well. That is also one reason why measuring activity alone can be so deceiving. The fact that there is a conversation does not tell you anything about the value of the content that was exchanged.

THE SUPER WATERCOOLER

One important element of knowledge management research has focused on the roles of story and narratives in sharing knowledge. David Snowden, first at IBM and later via his own company, Cognitive Edge, has been one of the key drivers of that line of thinking.[4] Also, Stephen Denning, former KM leader at the World Bank has written some books on organizational storytelling.[5] David, a great storyteller himself (I encourage you to look up some of this YouTube videos), has shown in his work that complexity cannot be approached using traditional methods, and that a lot of knowledge travels via the stories that people in an organization tell to each other.

A social media platform offers a great way to scale stories. What people are writing in some of those posts are not just bits of information, but many bits packaged into a story—*this is what happened, this is how I reacted, this is what happened then . . .* and so on. Even if a post is not an extensive narrative description of events, there is still often a hidden story that people start imagining based on the extract of the information as presented. In one of his early 1999 workshops, David taught me one thing about a good story that has stuck with me: A good story does not *tell* you the end of it. Just like how a good joke gets spoiled by having to explain the punch line, many good stories leave the conclusion somewhat open so the audience can read between the lines. As a result, the audience of a story will complete that element in their own way, in their own context, which will make the story's lesson much more personal than somebody else giving instruction about what to do next.

It is no coincidence that we humans usually like stories. Storytelling was the primary way knowledge traveled for many centuries before modern technology offered additional means and channels. If you look at the interaction of posts on a social network, it often resembles that of storytelling. An incident is documented (e.g., I have a problem with this feature in a piece of software); the person might try a few solutions independently and describe not only the outcome, but also the feelings that go with the different stages. Then, others give their advice as posts to the original question and there is an interaction, but there is always the story of the original poster working through an issue and the timeline of what happened. Of course for the original poster, a great ending to the story will be a solution (either one pieced together based on some tips, or one that somebody tells them directly). But for all the other participants, the benefit might not be that simple to describe. Someone reading that story might not get a direct answer to one of her problems, but instead get a description of a way to go about a solution. This might trigger a number of benefits, including learning a new way of thinking to use on a different problem now or in the future.

A social media tool that is specialized to deal with questions is StackOverflow, where the focus is very clearly on questions and answers and the rating of them through a community type of social behavior. But it might also spawn an idea for a more general solution. Maybe the developer of a piece of software that was in question is now thinking about how to avoid commonly discussed user issues in the next version of his software. No one has to tell him to fix this or that—it is his own knowledge combined with some key points in the social media story that trigger this new insight and enable action for the subsequent benefit of many.

You might have experienced similar types of stories around the watercooler or coffee machine in your office. But they can happen in almost all settings. Taxi drivers might share them with one another when waiting for clients; construction workers when sitting down with their lunch. But how do you enable the type of conversations that bring those stories to the forefront? An ESN is an infrastructure that might offer ways for more of them to happen across the whole organization, across sites and countries, and across departments—all constructs that have the potential of becoming silos. So an ESN can become what I call the super watercooler that potentially spans all those silos. I say potentially because there might be connections that don't make sense or conversations that don't happen on an ESN, and that's okay. It would be overkill if every employee was connected to every other employee and they were all engaged in active discussions. Such activity would overload users and actually reduce productivity, causing an ESN to be counterproductive. Yet the sheer possibilities offer great potential for learning and innovation.

The analogy to a watercooler fits in a number of ways. One of the misunderstandings that those new to social media have is that they have to digest what is happening exhaustively, and if they miss a bit they lose out. It might actually be true that they miss out, but that is not the point. You cannot stand in front of the watercooler or out in the hallway to catch every potential conversation that might get started there—it is the same with social media. Nevertheless going to the watercooler every once in a while and engaging in conversation with your colleagues or visitors can be a great value. Saying that you do not use a social network because you cannot catch 100 percent of the information is like saying you are never going to talk to anyone at the watercooler ever again because you will miss out on all the other conversations that happen when you are not there. Using social media tools is a bigger paradigm shift away from traditional email-driven cultures. This point is missed by many, especially those who judge social media without actively trying it out—this means going beyond looking at a few posts and determining that they are uninteresting.

HANDLING THE DYNAMIC ORGANIZATION

Organizations are getting more and more dynamic in a lot of ways. For one, structures of many organizations are changing more frequently. This might be due to product cycles becoming shorter, which lead to rearrangements of different parts of the organizations around those new products or solutions. Another reason can be frequent management changes. Some companies change their management almost as quickly as German soccer clubs change their coaches, believing that every stretch of low performance that lasts longer than the board would like means that it is time to bring in new ideas with new management. Every new manager brings in new ideas and that might lead to changes in the way the organization is structured.

Other reasons for more dynamic businesses are mergers and acquisitions. They extend the organization and also lead to combining some parts and splitting others. Outsourcing, near-sourcing, and extended partnering to various degrees create new ties and might change old relationships. All of those changes affect the way that staff in an organization interact with each other. In a lot of cases the changes mean change in proximity. Teams or team members get moved around and, let's face it, in some cases it does not make a big difference if one goes to a different floor or a different country. Out of sight, out of mind, as the saying goes. I once performed a social network analysis with a department moving within the same city from one building to another. The buildings were only a 10-minute drive apart, but the divide in dropping conversations was dramatic.

So when staff and the expertise they embody move around so much, how do you keep important conversations going? An ESN can be just the tool to do that. People might know each other well, but seeing a picture and what the other person does on a daily basis makes it a lot more likely they might maintain some of the old links. And that is not only a benefit for keeping old ties, but it is also a chance for building new links because there will be new conversations happening between the person that moved to another area and those in his new proximity.

A social network keeps track of the links between people, regardless of where they moved, whether their job title has changed, or if the department has been restructured. When it comes to conversations, it is not so much about those formalities, but more about the person at the end of that link, the knowledge she has, and the network she has built that can help others.

There are some other ways that an ESN can support organizational dynamics. Tags represent dimensions and build connecting elements between content in every imaginable corner of the social network; and tags are inherently dynamic as well. Any user can create one of those tags by simply putting an octothorpe (#) in front of a word and it represents a potential new dimension. Whether this dimension includes a good range of relevant content elements depends on factors like time, marketing, and evangelizing. But once the dimension grows through the network it provides value for finding content and connecting posts of a similar type. Just as hot topics and terms are changing ever faster in organizations, a social network can keep up with those changes.

In traditional, more static websites it would take a lot more effort (and time) to implement those types of categorization changes, especially with frequent updates by a community, but must be managed by a central group, which usually struggles with a bottleneck.

Groups are another entity supporting dynamics. In an ESN they are usually very easy to create (and also to delete), so users can create them as they like or need. Groups have been a very popular feature on The Hub at SAS, and within a year more than 900 groups (200 of them private) were created. As groups come and go they mimic the key topics that people are interested in at a certain point in time. And when things change, certain groups might become less popular while others are more prominently featured—another way of keeping pace with changing structures on the fly.

INNOVATION ENABLEMENT

Innovation is different from invention, as real innovation includes the application step. It is not enough to have a great idea or a new combination of ideas to produce value—successful application is the key step that is needed. Also true is that it is necessary to build a funnel of ideas that innovation can build on. It is a myth that inventors mostly sit in an isolated little room and come up with great ideas. Especially today, new ideas are based on collaboration and prior thinking, and emerge from smart combinations of old ideas to create new concepts that, in some cases, simplify on the way. Very often innovative strategies break a chain of thought by bringing ideas that might have worked in a completely different environment into a new situation to find ways to improve.

When discussing communities, I have heard people talk about the fact that some of the greatest innovations actually happen on the border of the communities. And I can relate to that point. Some of my best ideas have come from talking to someone in a completely different field who talked about concepts that I could transfer (to some degree) to a knowledge flow management issue.

This might happen when you get into some kind of meeting that brings diverse disciplines together, or it might happen when you sit at dinner with people from a range of backgrounds. But how can you instill this effect in an organization? Some organizations have created so-called think tanks, where they specifically bring together experts from different fields. In some cases they might actually organize specific events where experts from one division of a company are asked to collaborate with those from a completely different one. One example I have heard about occurred at a household product company that was having a problem with washing machine motors. They brought together motor developers from small household appliances like blenders with those from the washing machine division and were able to solve the problem collaboratively.

But what about the smaller-scale day-to-day improvements and innovations—those that you do not necessarily plan ahead? This is where the exchange that happens on an ESN can have a real impact. For one, more ideas come out, when a large group of people share what they do, what they struggle with, or what solutions they have found. This will help feed the funnel. Next is the diversity aspect. As long as people only engage in groups, the quality of their interactions will not be different from an exchange on a traditional mailing list. But a social network has those other dimensions to connect content and ideas. People can find content (i.e., ideas) through followers, tags, or by browsing their home stream of posts every once in a while. This means ideas are exposed to a lot more people of different cultures, backgrounds, and frames of thought.

An ESN can build a bigger, more diverse funnel of ideas, but there is one more important point that actually helps with innovation. The ideas are exposed to many people who can comment on them immediately, making every idea and post more of a conversation about a topic. This could result in critical voices and resistance, but for someone wanting to pursue it, this is not necessarily bad since it can encourage them to figure out how to improve on their initial idea. It could give the idea an immediate reality check. The response to social media criticism and feedback depends on how the innovator might deal with the arguments; he can ignore them or use them to refine his idea. If the vision is strong enough, the idea will survive. Without that type of exposure, a reality check is missing.

Another effect regarding ideas is that cautioning feedback and resistance often leads the idea creator to completely new solutions. Here is an example to illustrate the point: A few weeks ago my wife was watching a YouTube video on the history of Ortho-Bionomy® (a type of osteopathy/physiotherapy) that she practices herself and, as our desks are next to each other, I listened in a little. The narrator explained the history on how a doctor named Arthur Lincoln Pauls developed Ortho-Bionomy® as a new line of osteopathy. At one point, the narrator explained how Arthur found some new ideas presented in a paper by another osteopath named Lawrence H. Jones. Arthur played with the ideas, combined them with his expertise as a black-belt judoka, and further developed them. When he went to see Lawrence to present the evolution of the original line of thinking, Lawrence was not really interested—he said it was just not his thing.

Ever hit that point? Well one of two things usually happens then. Either you give up, or you believe enough in your idea to follow it yourself and go off and do your own thing. That is exactly what Arthur did; he gave it a new name (brand) and developed it into a method that he started teaching in 1976 and that thousands of Ortho-Bionomy® practitioners are using around the world today to help people ease pain or gain mobility.

What struck me about the story was that if Lawrence had been more open, the idea might have never really made it mainstream. The resistance that Arthur hit helped the innovation in some way. It was like a test to see if Arthur believed in it enough. You hear this quite often that great ideas went through a lot of phases of resistance before finally making it. Part of it is that resistance makes you think harder. That is why sharing ideas is good and keeping it hidden for fear of resistance is not.

I once had an idea for a collection of tools that would include not only plug-n-plays but also a whole range of quality, size, and types of other tools. When hitting resistance, I started the knowledge flow initiative ToolPool—and that was more than 820,000 SAS internal downloads ago.[6]

NOTES

1. "The New Conversation: Taking Social Media from Talk to Action," report by Harvard Business Review Analytic Services, 2010.
2. Gagen MacDonald and APCO Worldwide, "Unleashing the Power of Social Media within Your Organization," 2012.
3. McKinsey study, "How Social Technologies Are Extending the Organization," 2011, www.scribd.com/doc/79198468/McKinsey-Enteprise-Web2-0-Studie-2011, accessed May 29, 2012.
4. See www.cognitive-edge.com, accessed May 29, 2012.
5. The initial book I always recommend by Stephen Denning is *The Springboard: How Storytelling Ignites Action in Knowledge-Era Organizations* (Oxford: Butterworth-Heinemann, 2000).
6. ToolPool was the key case study discussed in my first book, *Mastering Organizational Knowledge Flow: How to Make Knowledge Sharing Work* (Hoboken, NJ: John Wiley & Sons, 2010).

CHAPTER 3

Getting Started

Things don't have to change the world to be important.

Steve Jobs (1955–2011), late Apple CEO

INSIDE VERSUS OUTSIDE SOCIAL MEDIA

Over the years, one trend I have observed, especially when it comes to web-based technologies, is the movement of tools from the external web to the internal workings of organizations. In fact, this is similar to a common strategy used by those who make the tools so successful on the external web. At first, they offer tools for free in order to familiarize as many users as possible with them. The hope is that these users will like the tools and company and come to rely on them on a daily basis. After that, most companies develop another tool—usually a low-cost alternative to the free one—that adds additional support, extended features, space, or throughput. Finally, companies usually offer some type of corporate version of the tool that promises to provide the same benefits that people get from it on the external web but within the privacy and focused environment of an organization. One early example is Google search. Google's general web search is and stays free, but Google now offers a whole range of features and services around search that are not free. In addition, on a corporate level you can get Google to supply you with an internal search engine that is focused on search within your organization and its websites and content. The strategy of offering several levels from free to fully paid has been so successful that recently vendors offer them right from the start of launching their product or service.

Another version of this process is a model where companies offering services might take an open-source tool that is available on the external web, where it is used by communities, and wrap the tool into a bundle that provides organizations a way to use the tool internally, within the confines of company borders.

Social media tools and platforms are definitely one class of applications that have successfully used those strategies to find users. The question is: How easy is it to replicate a tool's benefits on the external web within one's organization? There are definitely a number of differences between those two worlds—viewed from an organizational standpoint, you could call them the inside world and the outside world. In some cases, things are easier in the outside world, but in others the inside environment offers advantages.

At least at the start, it is usually the number of potential users that is dramatically different, of course. The next section will take a closer look at what that might mean to a social media initiative. But there are also often extensive differences between an organization's culture and that of the external web. Organizations are bound by different legal responsibilities, so they are often held more accountable for enforcing legal rules. As the external web spans so many legal zones it is a lot harder to enforce a common international set of rules and, as a result, it is often not so much about enforcement (other than strongly illegal acts, which are pursued across some country borders), but about guidance and individual behavior. A good example might be the sharing of pictures. While people are often open to sharing their personal pictures with others, an organization must obey the laws and regulations regarding personal pictures for every country it operates in. This sometimes makes it harder to support the consistent usage of pictures on an internal social media platform than it does on an external one.

There is another important angle to the difference between internal and external social media beyond just how those platforms are different at launch time. This is complicated by the fact that the two are beginning to merge in some respects. An internal platform that starts within the boundaries of an organization might well be extended to the outside and include collaboration and knowledge flows with partners and customers. In some cases, this might make it necessary to introduce additional options for privacy levels, but some content could be completely open to be discussed between organizational members and those outside. Social media platforms can become the basis for opening up collaboration with other entities on an ongoing basis, not just at certain partner meetings or customer events.

SAS has always tried to keep the communication channels between its customers and partners very open. Since the year of its founding, 1976, it has facilitated user group participation and open discussions, which are still being run every year. Additionally, in the last few years, social networks have been put in place to ensure that collaboration is an ongoing process that goes beyond the yearly meeting. The next step—and several organizations have done this already—is to run platforms that allow knowledge to flow across the organizational boundary, making partners or customers just part of those networks. As a result, the terms "internal" and "external" start to fade, as those notions are turning more into new dimensions of levels of access. For instance, a certain group that works on company strategies might only operate within the boundaries of the organization and not have any external participation; but other groups and communities can span different organizations. Some groups and features might be fully open to the public, while others are part of a specific subnetwork that includes only certain parties or purposes (e.g., all partners, customers, and employees working on a certain topic or development partnership).

DIFFERENCES IN THE WORLD

Now let's have a closer look at some of the differences between using social media in the external world and the internal world. It usually starts with scale. The social media platforms that we are most familiar with have been growing over years and reached user numbers beyond imagination. With almost 800 million[1] users on the planet, Facebook would be the third largest nation,[2] if social networks qualified. (Personally, I think that likening it to a nation is not fully appropriate, but for the purpose of size comparison, it is an interesting way of looking at it.)

Even if you take into account that not all of the 800 million accounts are active, and that in a given point in time you usually only reach a fraction of people, such large social networks are larger than any typical organization. There actually are some organizations with millions of employees and, in those cases, some of what I outline in this chapter might not fully hold; but for most organizations it is more about hundreds or thousands of employees than it is about millions.

Clearly, in terms of scale, a huge social network like Facebook—that is open to the entire world—has a lot more potential users than a 500-employee organization. To get collaboration going and to get a social media platform active, you usually need a certain number of users. The number of users who will be active is only a portion of the potential users. You could view the process of converting potential users to active users as similar to the sales funnel that converts potential buyers into active buyers. For a social media initiative, this could look like Exhibit 3.1.

If you are only looking at scale (we will discuss other factors later in the chapter), it seems natural that you might be more likely to reach a larger number of active participants when you start out with a larger

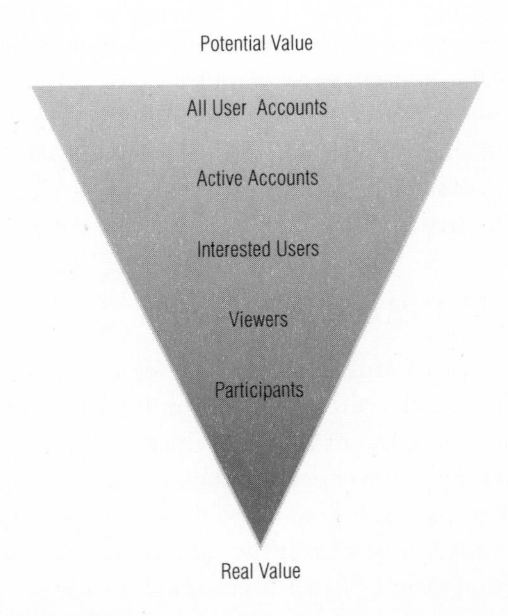

Exhibit 3.1 The User Funnel

number of potential users. In this case, the peak of your funnel at the bottom will actually contain more people as well. For real value creation in a social media platform, a certain number of people usually define a critical mass, depending on the type of social media tools you use. If your platform is about sharing diverse ideas, having only 3 people connected in one country bears less potential than having 8,000 connected across 50 countries. Communities have been said to have a good critical mass when they have around 100 members, but using fixed numbers for judgment is very hard, as it really depends on a number of different factors. For smaller, internal platforms this usually means you might have to work harder to reach critical mass. In an organization, you might have only five people discussing one topic, whereas there might literally be 100,000 experts around the globe that have that same passion. So, if you want an exchange with value in your organization's platform, you have to make sure you get all five of your people involved. On an external platform, if only 5 percent of the potential 100,000 will hop on your train, you are looking at 5,000 experts—a huge potential for exchange, learning, and innovation. Despite this challenge, there might be ways to get to higher participation rates that are not as easily available in the external world.

Another significant difference between internal and external platforms is the level of independence of users. Individual users out on the external web are usually more independent from each other. Most organizations have the potential to build a stronger social media community because their users are more likely to rely on each other. If we are talking about corporations, there is usually a hierarchical structure and, even if employees are independent in a lot of ways, there is at least that common management and strategy element that will build a framework from the top, down. In addition, an organization can execute certain strategies to increase participation, including having bonus and incentive plans in place for influencing members that support the shift in a certain direction. Independence has some upsides and some downsides. From an innovation point of view, independence can block group thinking and support greater diversity of ideas. On an internal network, you might still have great diversity, but only very large organizations can compete with the hundreds of millions of users out on the external web.

One goal of using social tools in organizations is to get input into decision-making and innovation via crowdsourcing.[3] The idea behind crowdsourcing is to get input from a large group of individuals, where each person has some information about a situation as well as a position on a situation or future outcome. Especially for future outcomes in the form of prediction markets, crowdsourcing is a growing tool to get additional information into the decision-making process. It is astonishing how often those crowd predictions are more accurate than the opinions of single experts. One of the requirements for the principle working, however, is a certain independence of the participants. If participants are influencing each other, the outcomes are usually not as good. Within an organization the chance that people know each other and influence each other is higher than if you are targeting an external audience. But a lot also depends on how people are organized and how they are targeted. The chances of running into independent crowds is higher; but even there, it is a possibility that those in the crowd have some kind of connection, belong to a certain community, and lose their independence that way.

Internal initiatives like enterprise social networks (ESNs) have the potential to be more controlled and directed. This might come from the guidance of executives or key sponsors, and it is likely that there is more influence possible via executive messages, internal marketing, or processes. However, this is also a big danger that could set an ESN up for failure. The social media platform is actually a tool to offer a balance for the more controlled environment of an organization. The moment participants have the feeling that they are being controlled, much of the value of collaboration and innovative communication will be destroyed very quickly. Careful guidance is one thing, trying to control the message is another, and those organizational leaders that think they can use a social network to control messages should be prepared to run into unexpected effects. Eventually, the users will realize the leaders' true intentions—to use social media for control—and might actually turn on them, though this would probably not happen openly on the social media platform.

An area where an ESN might provide an advantage is that of formal training—especially for software and systems. Training almost always comes at some cost. As an organization, this type of cost is usually planned as part of the individual development of employees. On the one hand, redirecting some of that effort into an effective ESN training program is potentially easier than producing and organizing it through an external module. On the other hand, a lot of learning and training happens on the platform itself via community help forums, and with the much larger potential community on the external web, it is often easier to get help there.

One word on motivation: One of the key activities in an ESN is contributing—and the contributions should be of high quality in order to create valuable interactions. If an organizational culture is right, it might be easier to market a feeling of unity and get a lot more people behind an effort. After all, a feeling of community and commonality drives ongoing high-value contributions because people are motivated to give their best. The variety of contributions might be bigger on a larger-scale network, but if conditions are right, the average quality of posts can be better. Good internal marketing to drive the message can go a long way, but it must also be a genuine message from the top that helps individuals see real value.

One common motive for contributing content to a social network lies in people trying to build standing and reputation. Within an organization, as people might know each other on many other fronts, this might be quite a different game than externally, where the chance is that individuals in the network do not know each other.

When it comes to technology, external social media networks need to scale effectively, as well. With a wider range and higher number of users, there is more chance that some of them will run into bugs or missing features more quickly and, at least for some of the more successful social networks, this means getting to stability in a shorter time. In contrast, internal social media platforms (at least if they are largely built with internal resources versus buying a platform off the shelf) might get less exposure and user testing. Also, the competition for features and stability is usually smaller within an organization. While on the external web people just move to the next best thing, internally there will likely not be a range of platforms to choose from. The question is more likely to be "Do I use it or not?" and not "Which one should I switch to?"

To drive a social network you might need some key stakeholders to embrace and push it. This should be easier to do on an internal level than with external social media. Influencing stakeholders (e.g., bloggers, technical consultants, press can be somewhat tricky and it needs to be done with extreme care. Such strategies could easily backfire if those stakeholders suddenly appear to be biased and clearly not independent.

One difference that seems counterintuitive is the way that legal conditions influence the development of a social network. The first reaction might be to think that this is more of a problem in the external world, but often it is within organizations that legal limitations play a role. On the external web, a lot happens without any overarching, international legal framework; however, on an internal platform the ownership of any personal data within an organization depends on government rules regarding the interaction between two parties (i.e., the organization and the individual). As an example, displaying employee pictures on a social network might require that every individual give consent; however on an external network, many people just decide to show their pictures without any hoops to jump through to allow such behavior. This is because often the legal framework is stronger when protecting individuals from third parties, as opposed to encouraging them to protect themselves. As a result, an organization may face legal issues and fines from just one single problem, and must create a deciding body to evaluate all possible problems. This deciding body is missing on external networks; regulations and limitations there are often decided, not by lawyers, but by the community itself, which can drive equally strong movements.

Another general difference between internal and external platforms could be the motivation of those driving them. Within an organization, the motivation is often to get full adoption by all employees (and, potentially, some external parties with selective access to the network). In contrast, external social networks usually have the goal to keep growing, until everyone on the planet with Internet access is a user.

Some network creators might actually just have the goal of reaching a critical mass that, while not enough to compete with social media leaders, is interesting enough to support a buyout or acquisition by a larger company. One recent case was Facebook's acquisition of a small app company named Instagram. Instagram is an app that allows smartphone users to take pictures, modify them to look historic, and then share them with their social contacts. The app was first published in the Apple App Store in October 2010. Only 18 months later, Facebook announced that they would take over Instagram for $1 billion. At that time, the small company had only 12 employees and no real business model. Their motivation was not necessarily to be bought by Facebook, but this can become a key motivation for others in the future. Those differences in business motivation can have a considerable impact on the value of the platform for users over time.

LAYING THE FOUNDATION

One observation I have made about the launch of our ESN at SAS is that it seemed as if a lot of people were waiting for it. For about five to six years, a growing number of people had engaged on external social networks (company policy specifically allowed this under certain guidelines), and there was more and more activity internally, as well. The first internal blogs at SAS were started around 2005.

Some managers took a little longer than others to get used to and endorse this new communication tool, but more and more of them opened up and started seeing the opportunities in blogging, despite some of the dangers they saw. After all, most potential pitfalls of such blogging usually never even manifest themselves at the level that social media skeptics might fear.

After the blogs, other tools like wikis and even an internal twitter application came about, all of them gaining more and more users. Those tools laid the foundation for a full ESN since they made more people used to social media tools and increased awareness of some of its unique aspects and benefits. Those early adopters were an important group as evangelizers and drivers once the full platform was rolled out.

At SAS, those first tools were not fully integrated with each other. Most of them were simple, from a technological point of view. The key was that it was easy to get your own blog, for example, and that the procedures did not stand in the way of sharing content. The first main focus was not on getting a homogeneous landscape of perfectly integrated tools—it was about experimentation and giving people an easy and quick way to try some things out within the internal organizational environment.

So when The Hub was finally launched, it wasn't like everything was new to a number of people. And those who had used the nonintegrated versions of different tools immediately saw The Hub as a positive step toward a more integrated platform, which had most of what they like about LinkedIn or Facebook to communicate with colleagues. They realized they could use it for work-related things that they might before have done over Facebook because there was no internal alternative.

This foundation helped with the launch, made internal marketing easier, and led to having a community of evangelizers that immediately got active promoting the new platform. On the one hand, as you get started with your own initiative to launch an ESN, you might have more aggressive plans to get it out, so waiting until people familiarize themselves with tools might not be something you can afford to do. On the other hand, if in the assessment of your organizational culture you feel there is still a lot of resistance, it might actually be worthwhile to take it slow on the full ESN and get started with some smaller initiatives (like blogs) first. This can be done with the very focused goal of getting people to experience the power of such tools. However, if you want to push ahead on your ESN, you should realize that building up a community of evangelizers will be a task you might have to focus on in the first phases, and that full adoption (when more people fully believe in the value) might take a little longer. It is easy to underestimate that point, but every knowledge flow management (KFM) initiative should start with the people. The technology is a great enabler, but without the growing buy-in of people, you will only get a fraction of the benefit.

The extent of social media savvy at SAS can be seen in the following story: About two weeks before the official launch was planned and about two weeks after a small group of early adopters was testing the new platform, I had some discussions with one of the project managers about The Hub. Suddenly the project manager received an email and said, "Oh, I think something just went wrong."

"What happened?" I asked.

She told me she had sent an email to one of the IT managers inviting him to have a look at The Hub and she had not clearly stated that it was still in testing and not for wider distribution at that point.

The IT manager actually liked it enough to send that email on. What happened in the next days can only be described with the word "viral." After one week, The Hub had over 1,000 users (including top executives, one of them even creating his own special interest group). The project team quickly took the ball and ran with it. Instead of trying to stop any of this, they took the momentum and built on it.

One of the reasons they wanted to start with the small test group was stability. As we were still making some adaptations on the system and processes, the system had to be taken down a few times, and it showed a few errors still. But as people seemed to really like it, the right solution was to just tell them what kinks were still being worked out. In turn, the internal communications group decided to launch an article on the Intranet (and of course cross-post it to The Hub) in which they officially invited anyone who was interested to become an early adopter. People very often really enjoy being in that role. Who doesn't want to be on the edge of developments? Along with that role, and those undertaking it usually understand this, comes reducing expectations of what they are getting. So, the article stated just that, outlining that there will be reboots, that some of the functionality might yet not be fully stable, and while the team will strive to provide good service, they would still be focused on stability changes versus wish-list features. Everyone was encouraged to use a special tag (#hubtesting) to indicate anything they did not like (e.g., errors, inconsistent data).

In hindsight, this was a brilliant move by the communications department. They harnessed the momentum and also managed expectations. By the time the official launch date came, 2,900 of 12,000 employees already had been going into the platform—a very fast adoption rate.

If you are launching an ESN in an organization that does not have as many social-media-savvy people who are open to the idea, your expectations should probably be somewhat lower and your effort for bringing it closer to them should be more concentrated and encouraging.

Apart from what we might call the "social media culture," there are other foundations that you need to create. An ESN will potentially affect a large portion of the members of your organization, so it is essential that you involve representatives from all potential groups in the planning phase. At SAS, about a year before the launch we started to bring together a diverse group of people that represented different departments like IT, internal communications, knowledge management (KM), research and development (R&D), webmasters, sales and sales support, technical support, legal, and any others that play a major role at SAS. We also included our work-life balance group. We then collected and scored requirements, at one point having a list of about 100. The group consisted of 30 to 40 people as well as some representatives from the regional offices. After all, it was supposed to be a platform for all SAS people, so we had to make sure that whatever we came up with would fit the Korean sales team as well as the U.S. technical support consultants. The lead was taken by an eight-person core group of members, which included the sponsoring communications department and IT. This process took about six months and was supported with regular phone conferences and also some smaller committees that investigated certain issues in more detail.

Only after this phase was over and we had agreed on a number of key starting requirements, did the group move to technology and start looking at different solutions. Functionality, time to market, integration capabilities, and price were some of the factors that played into the decision on the technology. This evaluation process took another few months and ended with the decision to choose a software platform from Socialcast by VMware.

This process and the discussions that took place turned out to be very important to ensure that everyone was behind the solution as much as possible. There were compromises, of course, and not everyone was completely satisfied to start with, but the vision was to accommodate other requirements in later phases, if they were still needed.

Another step that took place in the middle of the process was the creation of a communication plan that outlined when the project team would inform which parts of the organization about the new platform. One early point of that step was the naming of the platform. About five months before the launch, there was a competition so all global employees could send in their suggestions for names. Those suggestions, and discussion around them, were visible to everyone so a momentum built towards a certain set of them. Before the project team finally picked the final name from the top candidates, they took certain nominations off the list:

- Names that could lead to potential trademark violations.
- Names that might have sounded great in one culture, but had no (or misleading) meaning in other cultures.
- Names that were not fully politically correct.
- Names that were just too long.

One name that came up was "PROC Social," in reference to a key element of the SAS programming languages that deals with procedures (PROC, for short). This one was eliminated because it would have been too technical for many of the nontechnical employees. Another one that came up was "9 Cows," in reference to the fact SAS started out doing agricultural analysis that happened to be based on an experiment with nine cows. While this is a unique name, it would have not been easy to relate to unless you knew the story.

The short list was presented to all users for voting, and then the project team finally voted on the top three one more time.

The nice side effect of this competition was that months before the start of the platform, employees received regular information that something is in the works and that they can expect it fairly soon. With the nomination process and the commenting, it got them more involved in what IT usually does—provide additional input for the project team by helping to decide on a name. The degree to which people participated in the contest, defended candidates, or lobbied against them produced an involvement with the topic that was great for the momentum later. The winning name, "The Hub," was known by many employees way before it finally appeared on the sign-in page.

The name will define an internal brand and, as with any other brand, it is critical how it is launched and what people connect with it. This is a typical marketing method used to establish a connection to the value that an ESN might promise. Of course, it is important that the brand also deliver what it promises, so in building up to the launch and during the development phase it is important not to oversell it and promise features and benefits that are far out of reach, especially in the early phases. Social media tools live off the experience they provide, so it is better to let people make their own experiences than try to explain everything to them. From that point of view, the brand you will build might work better if it is not 100 percent specific, and instead operates on a more general level. If you get too specific, people will nail you down on those features and be disappointed when a newly launched platform is missing them. Keep in mind that the value and power is not so much in individual features, but more in the overall global connectivity that helps bridge silos in the organization.

The key lesson from the way that it worked at SAS is that it is good to have experimented with some social media tools before you even get started with a full platform. It is the experimentation that often starts out as a grassroots effort (often not 100 percent sanctioned, yet) that builds the breeding ground for more success later. In a 2009 study, Jakob Nielsen found that successful social media initiatives at the time started from underground grassroots efforts.[4] Recently, there have likely been a growing number of planned ESN efforts. Even in those cases it is probable that there was already some socialmedia activity going on, unless it was completely forbidden. If there was no support for it at all so far, moving quickly to a top-down setup will be a big challenge.

HOW TO REALLY GET IT OFF THE GROUND

In the previous section I talked about some of the pre-conditions for really getting started. Now let us have a look at what you really need for the launch.

Before you launch your ESN to your users, it is important that you have a team in place to guide it way beyond the launch. It is a common mistake to assume that after the launch all that will be needed is some technical support. If you want it to be a success, an ESN needs ongoing "initiative support," as I call it. There need to be at least a few people adapting strategies, guiding users, and organizing trainings (not just technical but also, more importantly, business trainings). Make sure you have identified this team and have set their roles accordingly before the launch. There is hardly anything worse than putting all that effort into the preparation only to risk your success by assuming it is a project that ends with launch day. See the next section for an extended discussion on viewing an ESN as an initiative.

For the actual launch it is important to use multiple channels to target potential users. In the case of The Hub, the main channel was our Intranet, where a number of articles highlighted the advent of the new platform and how people would be able to sign on. Earlier I mentioned the prelaunch spread of information about the ESN, which led to viral usage and a nice way of turning the preproduction launch into an early-adopter launch. In addition to this unplanned information spread, there were also a range of articles, videos, and webcasts to support the launch. The most active bloggers took the occasion to comment on the coming ESN and share their experience. Newsletters (e.g., one sent out by the knowledge office) highlighted "The Hub" and the importance it would have for the organization repeatedly.

Special initiatives included:

- A series of Hub tips, prominently featured on the company Intranet.
- The launch of a training website.
- Info booths in cafeterias during Love-The-Hub Day where a few project team members demonstrated the platform and offered employees assistance with the setup of their profile.
- Demos to executive leadership, including the company CEO Jim Goodnight.
- Activities around events that were moved to the virtual world of The Hub.

As I mentioned, there were already a number of people using other social media tools around SAS. Those were great candidates for helping to spread the word. For example, we used to have an internal Twitter-type system that more and more people had started using. It was called Chatter, and the audience was made up of research and development people on one side and marketing people on the other side. While it did not reach the stream speed of Twitter within certain groups, it did produce spikes of activity at times.

Very shortly after the launch of The Hub a number of users on Chatter pointed to the fact that they would be not posting there anymore because they were going to The Hub instead. People liked The Hub's range of additional functionality, so it was a very good replacement. Within a week of The Hub's launch, Chatter was practically dead, and a few weeks later the webmaster turned off the system.

It is important to note that Chatter was not forbidden or turned off while people were still using it. Rather people were lured to something better. This is very much in line with what happens on the external web with social media platforms. People sometimes move in swarms to platforms they like better or those that seem to be giving them more value. One example at the time of this writing is the growth of Google+. With 800 million Facebook users some people did not see how Google+ could have any chance of competing, but it is currently estimated to have reached 100 million users. In addition, in December 2011, U.S. analyst Paul Allen went as far as predicting 400 million users by the end of 2012 for Google+[5] (you will probably know whether it has become a reality by the time you read this book). The point is that at the current growth rates it is actually capable to become a serious competition. However, as individuals often have multiple profiles it does not necessarily have to mean that users abandon their Facebook profiles just because they start opening up a Google+ account. They can keep both and potentially use them for different purposes. One advantage of Google is a growing reach on the mobile market with the growth of Android mobile devices.

Most people do not appreciate being told that they must use this tool or that tool; they want to use the tool that best does what they need for their job—and maybe they want to use what everyone else uses, because there are always certain platforms that are considered cool. Users want to make these decisions for themselves, whether it's for work or personal use. It is not only an element of personal responsibility, but also personal individuality. Despite this, many users do want guidance. In the case of social media, this usually comes from peers and colleagues as opposed to a top-down mandate to use a certain system. This decision-making process is not completely new. I remember that when I launched my first knowledge management initiative, there was a competing initiative in the works at the same time. The people running the opposing platform requested that people use their system before they used mine. In the end, people went where they got answers. Even if you could force employees to use a system, if they don't believe that it provides value, they will probably not use it as intended and will create alternative processes. In the worst case, they might waste some time to make it appear as though they have spent time on the system, while, in fact, they still use whatever alternative channel they think is more worthwhile.

So how can you make it a no-brainer for people to regularly use a platform as one of their key tools?

I talked about the importance of marketing because it spawns engagement and can connect with people on many levels over time. It is necessary to use marketing to create what I refer to as the *pulse* of a knowledge flow initiative (KMI). Regular little campaigns to collect ideas can show the breadth and width of knowledge that exists in the organization. A great example of this type of campaign is asking a simple question to find a solution and, through the responses, generating several interesting, diverse, and innovative ideas. If one of those ideas is my own and it gets positive feedback, the end result is a positive experience of sharing, which will make me more likely to participate in future campaigns. Even those just watching will get an example of what can happen when strong minds unite. This strategy creates a transparent version of the idea-collection process, where there might have been more of a black box before.

Allowing groups and topics that are not directly related to business is another great idea to get a launch off the ground. Many organizational leaders fear that a social media platform can become a time waster and the possibility to discuss nonbusiness topics on an internal platform is seen as a way to make employees less focused and less productive. But let's be honest here: If, as a manager, one of your employees spends 80 percent of his time on a social media platform discussing hobbies and other non-core-business topics, then you don't have a social media problem—you have a management problem. It is an indication that the person is under-challenged and does not have clear goals and milestones. And, if he can reach his milestones and produce high-quality work even though he is spending that much time on the platform, maybe one of his hobbies actually makes him smarter about how he tackles business problems.

Letting those nonbusiness interactions happen is a great way to get some people interested in the platform. In fact, at SAS we have found that after some time, the discussion will actually turn towards business. We saw that with the way blogs developed. With blogs, employees were equally free to post whatever they thought might make sense. At the beginning, that included quite a few work-life topics—some people explained how they string a guitar; others talked about a weekend hobby. Nowadays, the blogs are almost completely business-related. You might have people leading with personal topics to make a post more appealing and interesting, but in the end it always turns into some type of business message. Part of the reason for this might be that employees have The Hub to catch some of those discussions. Over time, the business-related discussions will grow stronger than the nonbusiness-related elements, even though those will always be there and play an important role in getting people to use the platform.

One additional advantage to the inclusion of nonbusiness topics on company social media sites can be the positive feelings that some of the posts initiate. When I open up The Hub in the morning and I see some of the really amazing photography that my colleagues have posted in the Photography group that I subscribe to, the beauty of some of those pictures starts off my day with a positive feeling.

Similarly, the fact that some employees use humor (in a sensitive way and with the proper respect and cultural awareness) in their posts can be energizing. Some of the conversations—even some of the business-focused ones—develop into pieces that are a lot of fun to read, and a smile on your face can provide you with the boost of energy you might need at that moment. A daily dose of humor can make people more productive.[6] This turns the social network into a digital break room that helps reduce barriers and enables better communication in the long run.

Actually the tendency of moving from nonbusiness to business in conversations can even be seen in the company cafeteria. For example, in our Swiss office, there are often 10 or more people gathering for a coffee break in the morning (this is not planned, unless there is a birthday or anniversary cake there). Many conversations start out with "What did you do over the weekend?" or a question about an event or general news item. However, just as many conversations end with a work-related questions like, "What are you working on?," "Can we talk about this event/call/email . . .?" If people are busy and have challenging tasks, they tend to use any means to get the needed information. Running into someone who could help is more efficient than sending an email that might not be answered promptly because the other person is busy (though, luckily, not too busy for an occasional coffee).

This tendency is actually backed more generally by some studies of the use of personal devices in the workplace. In an Avanade study focusing on "consumerization of IT," it was found that there is a dramatic shift away from employees using mobile devices only for personal email and Facebook. These gadgets are now increasingly used for accessing mission-critical information and applications.[7]

As part of that study they also found that 40 percent of organizations allow employees to bring their own smartphones, 30 percent allow private tablets, and another 30 percent cover the full cost for these items.

A few weeks ago, I got the chance to take a tour at the European headquarters of Google in Zurich, Switzerland. What struck me was that in addition to the large lunch cafeteria, there were many small cafeterias, distributed throughout the building. All were a little different (ranging from a library to a jungle-themed room), always located near where people work; they all provided attractive settings with great coffee, soft drinks, and more but were small enough that people would actually interact, potentially more than in a very large open-space cafeteria as is favored by many organizations.

It is this type of atmosphere that one can mimic within an ESN using groups. We might be limited to create that physical environment for our organization in the short term, but we can create similar effects online. Once people see how this can make them more effective, you will have a growing number of adopters.

LAUNCH: PROJECT OR INITIATIVE?

In my first book, *Mastering Organizational Knowledge Management,* I spent quite a bit of time discussing the difference of a project approach versus an initiative[8] approach to get started with knowledge flow management.

Launching an ESN is a typical knowledge flow initiative, so most of what I discussed there holds true. The danger of looking at an ESN launch as a project is that, while it might get a good implementation at first, the long-term view is missing. Without this perspective all the cost and effort might be wasted. I can't spell this out often enough: This is not only about technology! It is about people! In turn, you will need an ongoing strategy and initiative support. You will need to invest in community management and training that goes beyond technology to cover business use. You will need a team to monitor the ESN on a daily basis so they can steer and guide it to function at a level beyond just answering users' technical questions. If you look at this with a project focus, you are only handling the first half of the game, and you are definitely risking the overall win.

Under the umbrella of a longer-term (multiyear) initiative you can run specific projects, of course—and one of those will likely be the launch of the ESN itself. Other typical projects under the initiative framework might include:

- Organizing an Innovation Day, where you collect ideas and later have a team evaluate those ideas and implement the best ones.
- An integration project that targets other resources within the organization and explores, defines, and creates integration points to make the platform more comprehensive and cohesive.
- Running regular requirements-gathering and revision-planning projects that will take the technical platform to the next level.

All those are valid projects, and it is likely you will have a few more, but you need to invest money in the people who run the show on an ongoing basis (e.g., community managers, trainers, and strategists). (We'll discuss more on this topic in the following chapters.)

TECHNOLOGY: BUILD OR BUY

The fact that this is the last section of the "Getting Started" chapter does not mean that it is not important. In fact, technology is where many people get started and then, unfortunately, never follow through with the initiative's other aspects—or at least not to the degree that they play an important role. There is no doubt the technology behind your ESN plays an important role; just don't fall into the trap of thinking that it's as simple as "if you build it, they will come."

One significant question about technology is whether you should build your own platform or buy a solution from one of the growing number of vendors. There are a number of factors that play into that discussion:

- In-house know-how and development expertise.
- Need for integration with existing and future systems.
- Cost for the platform and the ongoing support versus the development investments.
- Character of the vendor company (e.g., size, flexibility, cultural fit).
- Speed to market: It is usually faster to install something off the shelf than to start from scratch.
- Functionality: What do you get out of the box versus what are you capable of building.

This list is not necessarily complete, but it shows the importance of doing your homework. Do not jump into the decision just because one of your internal IT teams is keen on building you something or a key stakeholder saw a nicely staged demo and fell in love with it. It comes back to the need to do proper requirements-gathering first, and maybe also some prototyping.

SAS and Red Ventures both went with prepacked ESN solutions in the end. Red Ventures, which is considerably smaller, did not really have a lot of Web 2.0 tools internally before the launch of their ESN. Going with a standard solution was a great way for them to get started quickly. There were also some customization efforts that they put into it to really tune the system to their needs.

At first, SAS was tending towards an internal solution based on Microsoft SharePoint. However, some prototyping and close analysis revealed that, while the SharePoint platform was already available, it would have needed considerable investments to cover the collected requirements in a format that people are used to from external social media sites.

So in the end, SAS went with the ESN product from Socialcast by VMware. The simplicity of the platform was very appealing and the way that it was possible for a larger group, like the full SAS project team, to try it out via a hosted version really helped with a quick decision.

The installation within SAS took only a couple of weeks. Integration work with other platforms (including Microsoft SharePoint) is ongoing.

For SAS, the decision to go with an off-the-shelf solution was the right one, but it depended on multiple factors. SAS does have development resources at hand to customize and integrate the Socialcast ESN with other elements of the information infrastructure. In some organizations, integration might be even higher on the horizon. In addition, there could be other in-house applications already providing a migration path to social media functionality. As long as the effort to turn it into a platform with complete social media functionality is easier, faster, and more cost-effective than going with an off-the-shelf solution, it might be a viable way to go.

If you are starting from scratch and do not have any in-house web development or social media expertise, I would recommend looking at off-the-shelf solutions to determine how they match your collective requirements. Be careful not to overestimate the importance of certain features, though. The key question is whether that feature will endanger overall success if it isn't there. If the answer is yes, then ask yourself whether the product can be customized by you or the vendor to add those key features. Maybe it is already on the vendor's roadmap. If it is important for the success of an ESN, chances are, it is on their radar. If it does not turn out to be mission-critical, it might be best to drop it in the interest of simplicity. Technical people sometimes suffer a bias regarding the importance of certain detailed features that are not as important to general users, and in the end you are building an enterprise-wide platform that needs to appeal to technical as well as nontechnical people but technical people are likely to be the early adopters.

NOTES

1. Internet World Stats, www.internetworldstats.com/facebook.htm, numbers current as of December 31, 2011.
2. According to the *The World Factbook*, published by the CIA, China is the largest country, with 1.3 billion; India is said to have about 1.2 billion people, followed by the United States with 313 million. For more see: www.cia.gov/library/publications/the-world-factbook, current as of February 2012.

3. See James Surowieki, *The Wisdom of Crowds: Why the Many Are Smarter Than the Few and How Collective Wisdom Shapes Business, Economies, Societies and Nations* (New York: Doubleday, 2004).
4. Blog entry: Jakob Nielsen's Alertbox, August 3, 2009, www.useit.com/alertbox/social-intranet-features.html, accessed May 30, 2012.
5. See: Samantha Murphy. "Google+ Sees Massive Membership Growth," Mashable, 1/3/2012. Available at: http://mashable.com/2012/01/03/google-growth-2012/ and Ted Thornhill. "Google Plus 'will have 400m users by the end of 2010" – Will it overtake Facebook?" Daily Mail Online, 12/30/2011. Available at: www.dailymail.co.uk/sciencetech/article-2080207/Google-Plus-hit-400m-users-overtake-Facebook.html. (Both accessed May 30, 2012.)
6. FISH! philosophy, a consulting firm specializing in motivational techniques, includes the two key instructions "Play" and "Make their day," both of which are driven by fun and humor. See www.charthouse.com, accessed May 30, 2012.
7. See Tyson Hartman, "Debunking Six Myths of the Consumerization of IT," IDG Connect, February 17, 2012, www.idgconnect.com/blog-abstract/464/tyson-hartman-global-debunking-six-myths-consumerization-it, accessed May 30, 2012.
8. Frank Leistner, *Mastering Organizational Knowledge Flow: How to Make Knowledge Sharing Work* (Hoboken, NJ: John Wiley & Sons, 2010).

CHAPTER **4**

Roles

Do not worry about holding high position; worry rather about playing your proper role.

Confucius (551–479 BC), China's most famous teacher, philosopher, and political theorist

MORE THAN JUST SOCIALIZING

Whether you call it *knowledge management* (KM) or *knowledge flow management* (KFM), it contains the word *management*, which indicates that someone takes an active role. As I outlined in *Mastering Organizational Knowledge Flow*, an initiative to increase the flow of knowledge does need special attention. It is just not enough to communicate that knowledge sharing is part of everyone's role, and then assume it really happens. There are too many barriers that hinder the flow and it needs one or more dedicated people to help to reduce those barriers. With some initiatives the need for those roles seems more obvious than with others.

Social media platforms on the Internet appear to many as if they run all by themselves. The impression is that they were created in a true if-you-build-it-they-will-come fashion. This view is clearly underestimating the amount of support, strategy, marketing, and more that people in certain roles have put into a platform before it goes viral and reaches critical mass. Looking at enterprise social media platforms is no different in that sense. In fact, since the expectation for almost 100 percent adoption is a lot higher within organizations, the need for certain people to take an active role in moving it forward is even more important.

As mentioned in Chapter 3, external social media platforms and enterprise social networks (ESNs) have different characteristics and, therefore, might have to be handled slightly differently. On one side, it feels easier to interact with users on an ESN, as you probably have a better idea who and where they are, what they are interested in, and some indications of their culture (in this case, that's also the company's culture). Depending on your organization's existing communication processes and infrastructure, an ESN could provide a better chance of reaching users. Many traditional communications channels do not guarantee that your message is getting through.

A successful ESN should aim to spread across the organization, as that offers the potential of learning across regional boundaries, divisions, and communities. Wide usage also increases your chances of a high adoption rate. This is good because you want everyone who can potentially contribute to the knowledge flow on the ESN. However, different people are motivated via different drivers,[1] so you will have to find and continually fine-tune how you bring people into the ESN. Attendance is not enough since, in the end, you want people to engage and, in turn, create business value based on collaboration and interactions.

To ensure ongoing value, it is essential that you have a strategy that includes measures in place to see whether the ESN is generating the business value that you were hoping for. While socializing alone is an attracter, it is not where the value is. Only when those social activities create learning, can people get concrete help with business problems or discover new ideas that end in innovations that create business value.

For that reason it is essential that you have an infrastructure in place—and not just a technical one, but one that includes supporting roles. One key role is that of a strategist. It is important to note that the strategist role is filled not only to support the ESN's launch, but also afterwards, when it becomes an ongoing position. The platform will change, your users will mature, and their needs and wishes will change with their level of maturity—and a strategist will be a key player in navigating these challenges. An organization that is just starting with social media will have different expectations than someone who has worked with those types of tools and platforms for several years.

Another important role is that of a sponsor. Often ESNs start out with some social media tools that are introduced by the IT department for people to play with to get a feeling of what social media is all about. At that point, you might need a really good sponsor—other than an IT manager—that will allow people to spend a little time on these activities, which are often seen as exploration or research. However, if you are shooting for a full, enterprise-wide platform there might be considerable costs involved, especially if you take ongoing roles seriously. At that point, you will need an executive sponsor to advocate the cause.

As an ESN can develop into a major collaboration and communications tool, buy-in needs to come from the very top, and the main driver should have a clear interest in enhancing internal communication. Consequently, a good sponsor might be in corporate communications. The head of corporate communications, in case such a function exists, should have a great interest in new ways of enhancing communications and the degree to which employees feel informed. But sponsoring does not mean being the sole leader of the initiative. It is still important that IT, HR, many lines of business, and other stakeholders are part of the planning and rollout. Corporate communications might be able to bring the different parties together, including top management, behind the initiative. This is the route we took at SAS, and it worked out very well.

Beyond the sponsor role the communications department can also play another important role—that of marketer. This is another central role that is essential to ongoing success. Marketing—whether external, with a focus on highlighting products, or internal, as a means to drive behavior—has the goal of showing people the value of buying a product or buying into a concept or behavior. If people do not see the advantages of having a social media platform, they might be reluctant to participate. Once they do participate they often understand the value, but it is necessary to get them to the stage of trial. In later phases, there might be issues with it and that is where marketing needs to facilitate reposition, highlight improvements that deal with the issues, and point to tips and training that can improve any experience that might have been negative for some users.

For the operational phase of the ESN, there is one role that is of central importance, and the best name I have found for it is "community manager."[2] This term has been used in the past for those leading a community of practice (CoP) or multiple CoPs. The community manager (CM) of an ESN is focused on every aspect of the platform, including those users that might not be organized in CoPs yet. The CM looks at the bigger picture of the platform (and might also play the strategist role), but on the other side, the person executing that role will also need to participate on a detailed day-to-day activity level.

Typical tasks might include looking out for those users who have issues, defining and monitoring certain tags, and helping people very concretely with advice or pointing them to those that might be able to help. This could also mean pointing people with questions to the proper communities/groups, letting them know that they could join to get ongoing help with the questions they post. One other activity would be to suggest follower relationships to people and point them to usage tips, if it seems they are not using the platform efficiently. The CM would also be a good person to monitor statistics on the ESN and highlight them to the right audiences, which could include the sponsor as well as the user community. Growth numbers can be used to extend and build the momentum, for example.

While a CM should be an enthusiast who focuses on providing a positive spin around the ESN, she should also be proactive in managing stakeholder expectations. On a day-to-day basis, she should look for issues, but highlight the positive aspects, thanking people for special contributions. The CM position should have some constancy—if the person behind that role changes frequently, it will be a lot harder to produce some traction. After all, the CM is constantly learning and adapting processes along the way. This type of experience would be largely lost when the turnover in the position is high, so make sure you find a person who is likely to stick to it for an extended time (measured in years, not in months).

While a CM may post on the platform, in that role it is important to stay neutral. They should not take strong sides on issues or polarize discussions, but rather leave that role to others. A CM can stir things up by encouraging open communication, though. The focus of a CM is managing and facilitating—they should not get bogged down publishing others' posts and content because other people don't feel they have the time. If at all possible, no one, not even the CEO, should have a ghost-writer for the ESN. Messages should be short, and even a busy executive will find time to write a short sentence in the course of the day.

A general goal for the CM should be to bring additional activity from the offline world into the virtual world of the ESN. There are always those things that are much more effective in the offline world, but to strengthen the ESN's roots at the early stages, it is important to integrate both worlds more closely, and that usually means moving some activities over to virtual. One advantage of doing that is transparency and recordkeeping. If I discuss something that would be interesting to a wide audience in a private chat or on the phone, it is not as transparent and might result in some missed opportunities for learning and innovation.

Another important task of a CM is to encourage certain users to play their role as evangelizers, another central role. Evangelizers are usually well connected within the organization and they are the ones that can lead to a tipping point of usage.[3] But to become real evangelizers, users themselves have to become convinced of the ESN's value. In the reverse case, users might be the ones spreading negative sentiment on the ESN efforts. The best candidates for playing evangelizers are those who have already had good experiences with external social media platforms and also have sufficient knowledge of the corporate culture to understand how to position what might be new in a way to satisfy the people around them. Once they are convinced of the ESN's value, they can use the network and their strong social and communication skills to get others onboard. Sometimes all it takes is a single story to make others believers. The difference between central marketing (as done by corporate communications, top executive sponsors, or even the community manager) and the one-on-one selling that an evangelizer might do is the trust element. Often, over the years, evangelizers have built a trusted adviser relationship with many of their colleagues, who want to hear what they have to say. (We'll learn more about evangelizers later in the chapter.)

When we talk about roles, we should not forget the general users themselves, of course. Nobody can *make* them use the platform, so a lot will depend on their openness and their ability to manage an additional communication channel, and whether it will be possible to mobilize them. Their managers play a related role, either encouraging usage or reacting very cautiously, often driven by the fear that their people will get distracted from "real work" by using it. In a way, both of those roles include a certain type of sponsorship as well. Managers will sponsor activity by encouraging their employees to spend time on the ESN, and the individuals act as sponsors by choosing to spend their time on the platform.

If you are coming from the more technical view of knowledge management, you will definitely be missing one role by now: the role of technologist. It is an important role, but one needs to be careful not to spend all the money on that person and not have any left to pay for the marketer and community leader. Technology does play a role and, in the case of an ESN, it is important that you can react quickly on issues and requirements. You need a smart technical team that is focused on giving users just the functionality they are looking for.

That means the technologist needs a real customer focus. If he is too much in love with the technology, he might offer a lot of features that he, as a technologist finds cool and important, but new users find distracting and uninteresting. If even parts of an ESN seem too complicated to use regularly, nontechnical users might take that as a cue to never come back again. It is essential to remember that while the evangelizers and drivers might be technically savvy, the majority of your audience will often be anything but technical, especially if technology is not at the core business of your organization. Even at SAS, a company with plenty of technology-savvy people, many people have jobs focusing on nontechnological aspects, like sales, custodial services, or gardening. In the end, you want a platform that works for all members of the organization, so less can often really be more.

This is not to say that a good technical team is not essential for your success. A well-working stable platform is key to acceptance.

The role of the technology group does actually depend very much on whether you build your own system in house or whether you buy an ESN off the shelf and adapt it (see Chapter 7 for more on the discussion "Build vs. Buy"). If you build the platform yourself, it needs a team with considerable experience with ESNs (and hopefully they have read books like the one you are reading now). It can be a major project to try to recreate a feature you see on Facebook in a simple and stable manner on an ESN. You really need some top developers who can be very flexible and, almost instantaneously, add new features as requested by the users. Speed is essential.

However, if you buy an ESN from a vendor, it takes technology-savvy people with a good understanding of social media features in the evaluation and test phases. They must be able to really understand how that new platform will fit into the landscape and try to anticipate how diverse target audiences would use it. Usually the anticipation is limited, as there is always something that people will do with your ESN that will surprise you. When a platform is bought externally, the technology team will often play the role of an intermediary. You will not usually have many programmers on staff, unless the platform allows for detailed customizations. Your key technologist will need the profile of technical project manager, something you also need with an internally built platform. The intermediary role will be between the ESN vendor, the sponsors, the power users, and evangelizers as well as the wider user group.

I have seen a number of examples where a vendor ESN was used, and the technology group is astonishingly small. Even with a network of 10,000 people 2–3 technologists (sometimes not even 100 percent dedicated to the ESN) were enough to get the initiative off the ground and running. Well-designed ESN platforms are simple and just provide a framework; the power lies in the activity of the users and not in the number of features. This keeps system complexity down and does not make it necessary to have a huge group of technical people to support it.

Once the platform is in place and launched, the biggest technical efforts are usually concerned with integration. Disintegration presents one of the major barriers for people not using your ESN, or at least it annoys them to have to deal with multiple nonintegrated systems. So for user satisfaction, it is important to strive for integration. It is an ongoing process, where you might start with integrating user data, but later move to integrating with a lot of other systems, one by one. At that time, efforts become somewhat higher and you will also need to involve technologists from those other systems.

Whether you build or buy, the key for a well-received ESN is a certain amount of progress. This does not mean adding features for the sake of something new, but it means closely watching the needs of users and giving them what they need when they need it.

Good ESNs come with a lot of features out of the box, but they should also have a number of configuration and extension options (i.e., an Application Programming Interface, API) that a good technology team will be able to use to make progress and keep up with the growing maturity of their users and new requirements identified by the strategist.

INDIVIDUALS AND DEPARTMENTS

Most of the roles outlined in the previous section are individual roles, even if held by multiple individuals in a team. But there is also a role that complete departments can play. By identifying the ESN as a key tool in their communication strategy, they can motivate whole groups of people to move to it and use it as the primary tool for communication and knowledge sharing. One example might be the research and development department that realizes the value of ad hoc sharing of knowledge and widely encourages their team members to share their ideas. Another great example would be the group of external social media specialists, those that focus on social media as it applies to external representation of an organization. This is a group that is usually quite familiar with social media and, by using internally what they preach externally, they can get even more experience, create awareness of their external activities, and become a driver for the internal platform in general.

One danger with whole groups moving to the platform is that they just replicate the organizational structure in ESN groups. While it is understandable that people think that the unit "organizational group" would be good to have, very often those represent the silos that the social media platform is trying to break down. Over time, it becomes somewhat questionable what is being discussed in a group named "Sales Support France." Yes, there might be some guidelines, rules, and news that are worth sharing within that group, but I would argue that the higher value lies in discussing cross-organizational topics instead. So, it would be more important to talk about a product, a solution, a technology, and so on. And getting together all those people who have knowledge on any one of those types of entities (not bound by a country or department) raises the chances that silo-breaking knowledge-sharing is actually happening. The diversity of views is likely to be higher when Australian consultants and Norwegian consultants discuss a solution than if it is always only two Australian or Norwegian consultants, apart from the fact that some local organizations might actually only have a single expert on a given topic.

Another group that can play an important role is that of the middle managers. Individual employees will need a trusting manager that will agree that spending time on the platform will be of benefit to them. Behind this type of trust is a certain type of culture that enables employees and allows them to make their own decisions on how they get to solutions for problems. It takes managers that clearly define the framework and goals that their staff should be striving for without prescribing too much process on how to get there. Social media tools, regardless of whether they are internal or external, sometimes have the reputation of being pure distracters, especially with some more traditional managers that have not even tried and experienced them. It is easy to underestimate the power that comes from picking ideas and solutions from a larger crowd.

Managers need to be open to the idea and endorse sensible usage of the ESN. In fact, they could take a leading role, familiarize themselves with the ESN, and serve as a role model on how to use it effectively. After all, it offers managers an equally powerful platform to learn and exchange on management issues. At SAS, one of the most popular groups is the one where people exchange ideas, best practices, and articles around leadership and management. The message is that the platform can be an enabler, but it is, of course, not a guarantee that the employees will use it. They will need to believe in the value themselves, as well. Not having the discouragement of a disbelieving manager can reduce a barrier, however.

A group we should not forget, that should be involved early in the planning as well as on an ongoing basis, is the legal department. They often have the reputation of slowing things down and limiting freedom. Nevertheless it is very important to get them into the boat early. It is a lot more frustrating if they completely stop your initiative after finding out that things are not compliant with some legal rules or country laws. An ESN often spreads across multiple countries. In fact, larger multinational organizations are often getting the biggest benefit out of social media platforms. As a result, it is very important to build the ESN with an international view when it comes to rules and regulations. What can be done with personal data, for example, does differ widely between the United States, Germany, and China, for example. By ignoring those facts, you are setting yourself up for bigger headaches later.

Luckily, there is a growing number of lawyers that do have the experience with and knowledge of new technologies needed to work on optimizing the balance between being legally correct and flexible/usable. Yes, it will be a compromise and, in some cases, it might be frustrating to not just do what you think would make the most sense, compromising usability and functionality for some ridiculous law. Usually when you look closer and try to understand it from a local cultural perspective, you might see that there are very valid reasons why this or that country might have stricter privacy laws, for example. On one hand, it could be part of their history to be more fearful of authorities controlling them. On the other hand, another country could be in such a boom phase that they do not cling to history and for them everything seems valid as long as it brings progress.

So getting that legal advice early (even in the requirements-gathering and decision-making process) is essential to create and understand the framework that everything must operate in. Having such a framework from the start will make it a lot easier to safely operate within it.

An ESN is about people. So we should not forget one department that, by definition, deals with people issues in your organization: human resources (HR). The role of HR can happen on several dimensions. First of all, HR can play an active role in communicating with staff via the ESN. Information around HR topics are usually quite popular with people. A lot of the questions will be of a personal nature, but often there are things that are more general and apply to a larger group of employees, or even the whole organization. In case it is something that people must know, by all means, HR will usually use another channel that is guaranteed to reach people.

But often HR has to share some information that is not mandatory but would be valuable if more people were to make use of it. In that case, an open forum on an ESN is a great way to spread that type of information, to get a discussion going, and get a feeling of what people think about it. Good HR managers try to always interact with the staff they are responsible for. In smaller organizations or smaller offices of larger organizations, this can be done by walking around and talking to people (in fact that is what our local HR manager at SAS frequently does). With larger distributed teams and HR responsibility spanning multiple locations, this becomes a lot harder and, on the top level, it is even harder to get a feeling about where things are standing, what the current people issues are, and whether there is a certain type of cultural or mood-shift in the organization.

This is where an ESN can be of high value to the HR department, but they need to get involved and trigger some of the discussion. At SAS, for example, one of the most popular groups is the one about leadership development, clearly an HR topic. What is interesting is that the main contributors are a mixture of HR leadership development coaches and staff from the field that is passionate about leadership. And you can see from the roles of those posting that there is also a mixture of managers as well as nonmanagers. The latter are often those that strive to become managers or those that see leadership as something that exists beyond management. In fact, a number of the posts I have seen recently are precisely pushing that latter idea—that anyone can become a leader—and the ESN or blogs are good platforms to lead, even without official management authority.

Another reason why HR will have a vested interest in the ESN is the need for communication. It seems the majority of issues with people somehow come always back to miscommunication. And an ESN is a tool to enhance communication. Many times miscommunication occurs between a manager and their direct reports, and while those issues will not move to an ESN, they can also be solved in direct communication. But the cultural change that comes along with an ESN will change the relationship between managers and employees over time. Managers might not like it, but an ESN will give their employees more of a voice outside of their direct relationship, offering them more options to connect with others and raising the chance that they can move within the organization. By having easier ways to build their network they receive the "power of the foot." It is not always good to just walk away if things get tough, but in some situations it is a lot better than draining energy from the employee and the manager.

The workforce is changing constantly, and diversity, be it age or cultural, is something that all organizations have to deal with. An ESN presents a chance to get people out of their silos, whether the silos are built based on age, location, department, and so on. One of the commonly mentioned issues in organizations these days is the loss of knowledge due to a large number of employees retiring in the next decade. Often, the expectation is that HR deals with this fact and somehow makes sure the knowledge stays when those people leave. Traditional knowledge management methods would go along the lines to have them document as much as possible before they depart. While some documentation might not be a bad idea, this is not even capturing the tip of the iceberg, as the real value (deep) knowledge cannot be documented easily, but has to flow in the sense that other people really have to learn and create it as their own knowledge over time. This could happen via apprenticeship, storytelling, task shadowing, and other methods, but those do take time. Coming from a knowledge-flow perspective, the best way to keep knowledge is by embedding it into the brains of others as well as the expert you might lose.

This is where the ESN comes into play, as it can connect older experts with young new starters across the whole organization on a daily basis. Their knowledge (if you can get them to see the power of sharing it by posting information, leaving comments, or engaging in discussions) can spread a lot wider than if they share it only in a single engagement or project. In fact, it would be a good strategy for HR to ensure that older (near-to-retirement), highly experienced employees get more time to spend on the ESN and leave their knowledge with others, from old-time peers to those young professionals that came from university and just started yesterday.

A well-run ESN with HR support could be one of the best answers to the knowledge-drain problem.

So far, all the mentioned roles have been targeted at the scenario that the ESN operates only within the enterprise, but a growing number of platforms of that type are opening up and including partners or even customers on their ESN. Some content has special access rules for certain people, of course. But the dividing line is often not between inside and outside the organization anymore; it is more around certain topics. For example, you could have a private group that includes partners, customers, and employees, but only a small subset of employees that are allowed to have access to information around a given project. This book in large parts talks about inside the organization, but with borders between companies becoming more fluent and flexible, this view is limited if we think of an organization only as the traditional company. Using the wider view of organization, including those interactions with partners and customers, much of what is said here still applies.

Partners and customers might have different levels of engagement with the rest of the organization. You will discuss certain strategies with your partner differently than with your customers, especially in an early sales phase, but if you want to win long-term customers you will want to try to create a win-win partnership with them. To create that type of relationship, communication is key and a social networking platform (like an open ESN) can create a channel for ongoing communication, creating trust, building transparency, and building relationships between different parties.

The importance of that type of interaction is, of course, not new. From 1989 to 1993 I worked at a computer company called Pyramid Technology, which produced large-scale multiprocessor super-mini computers, and my employer Siemens-Nixdorf resold those computers under an OEM agreement. For quite some time I was the only Siemens-Nixdorf employee within Pyramid. I was sitting in the middle of their development team, however. I had access to people and resources and we even sent little instant messages via UNIX to each other. Building trusted relationships was the only way that I could do my job effectively (which for the first nine months was to merge two UNIX operating systems line-by-line).

But today's partnerships are much more fluid (i.e., cross-company teams build and resolve quicker), more international (location of those people building the partnering team can be literally anywhere on the planet), and often made up of a lot more people on both sides, as the 1-to-many relationship I had with the development team at Pyramid.

Partners and customers can play an important role in your ESN, as they bring an outside perspective. Correctly speaking, the question becomes: What is outside and what is inside, really? But they bring a perspective built based on their experience, which is likely to be quite different. After all, different perspectives, know-how, and capabilities are very often why organizations go into partnerships in the first place. And learning from your customers as fast as possible is a requirement to come to successful solutions for complex business problems.

MOBILIZE YOUR EVANGELIZERS

The first followers are just as important as your leaders. There is a really great video from TED, an initiative that invites those with innovative ideas to give a short presentation, where Derek Sivers presents how movements really get started.[4] In the video, Sivers shows some footage of a person starting to dance wildly, only to end up being surrounded by thousands joining him in the dancing. The key point Sivers makes is that the leader is not the key to making it a movement—the first follower is at least as important, if not more so, to really make it work. Another lesson learned from the video is that the leader needs to embrace the first followers as equals, giving them attention and gratuity instead of getting stuck in their own importance as a leader. Sivers calls it the "underestimated form of leadership of the first follower." This is one of the keys for how you should look at your evangelizers and turn to them for helping you get your ESN off the ground.

One idea to get others involved is to organize them in a group (CoP) on the platform to give them a chance to provide input and actively influence what is happening with the ESN. As those evangelizers are usually social-media-savvy, they could use existing channels to push the new platform. If, for example, some of them are already among your key internal bloggers, their blogs might be an ideal tool to reach a wide number of potential adopters.

Another method to get the message across using evangelizers is to publish interviews on the internal news channel with them, where they state their honest views of the new platform, why they participate, and where the benefits and potential dangers might lie. At SAS, the hundreds of bloggers were directly contacted, asked to check out the new platform, and share their experiences.

Another great activity to reduce fears and misconceptions is the organization of fairs. These are live events happening in a central, high-traffic location on a company site—maybe the entrance of the cafeteria where people pass to get food, or the atrium of a larger building.

The fair should consist of a number of desktop stations staffed with some experts or evangelizers who invite those passing by to have a look at the platform. They could also help them log in and set up a profile on the spot. Some people just need this direct experience to get started. The hurdle of doing it alone in their office is too big for some people. The encouragement during a fair is what could make the difference for them.

One last word on the general role of evangelizer. The word stems from the Greek word euangelion,[5] which was used to indicate a reward for good news given by a messenger and later used in the sense of "bringing good news." For quite some time it was primarily used in connection to religion. The *Merriam-Webster* online dictionary defines an evangelist (apart from the religion-based definition) as an "enthusiastic advocate," and, more and more, evangelism has been used to describe the way that messages of all kinds are distributed by a person. Within organizations, it usually does have a positive connotation to it.

So you should view your evangelizers as those who really internalized the positive aspects of your social network and are convinced enough about its value to spread the word to others. The way that happens is often via storytelling, which could be through talking to those they meet in passing, but also in the form of written stories, nowadays often expressed in the form of blog posts, as pointed out earlier.

The key fact is that the good news must meet a certain need. Very often, the message does not get across as the person to be evangelized might only see some of the negative impacts—like potential overload. I have had this type of discussion more than once. People have made up their minds based on external social media platforms and base their judgment on some high-profile cases (widely focused on by press and word of mouth) that, to many, show the negative or useless sides of social media activity. But beware, just because there might be a lot of stupid, apparently time-wasting things happening on a social media platform, it does not mean that everything there is a stupid waste of time. It really depends on how the tools are being used. Evangelizers need to work on the potential value proposition and open the mind-set of those they target to, at least, get them to the stage where they will try it long enough to really build their own judgment. Some tips on how to use it can help getting to that value stage. As I pointed out several times, social media is still a tool, and it can be used in many ways. It is amazing that by participating and trying it, often they find the value for themselves. It is hard to anticipate what people do (or not do) with a platform tool like this. You can give examples, but in the end users often—if they keep an open mind and want to learn—find ways to make use of the platform that even an evangelizer has not always anticipated.

To close this chapter I would like to summarize the main roles split into individual roles and group/department roles. For this purpose, see Exhibits 4.1 and 4.2.

Individual Roles	Function
Executive Sponsor	Fund, endorse, highlight
Community Manager (CM)	Strategize, market, guide, support (users), gardening, stir up, highlight, broker, connect
Evangelizer	Market one-to-one and via channels, generate followers, tell stories, spread the word
Individual Users	Post updates (ideas, links, pictures), read, comment, "like," create groups, repost, evangelize
Technologist	Translate requirements, develop, tune, integrate, support (technical)

Exhibit 4.1 Individual Roles

Group/Department Roles	Function
Corporate Communications	Lead, strategize, coordinate, market, tell stories, train
Human Resources	Train, position, utilize, encourage top experts, create guidelines
Executive Management	Endorse, participate (post, comment)
Line Management	Communicate, lead, show support, create priorities
Knowledge Flow Management	Evangelize, connect other roles, train, highlight, lead, drive
Information Technology (IT)	Provide technical infrastructure, integrate, communiate with vendor
Legal	Create legal framework (guidelines and policies), consult, highlight issues
Partner/Customer	Ditto Individual Users

Exhibit 4.2 Group/Department Roles

NOTES

1. For effect of drivers, see Frank Leistner, *Mastering Organizational Knowledge Flow: How to Make Knowledge Sharing Work* (Hoboken, NJ: John Wiley & Sons, 2010) 71ff.
2. "Community Manager" is the term that Philips used for the person running their internal, 29,000-person social media platform.
3. See Malcolm Gladwell, *The Tipping Point: How Little Things Can Make a Big Difference* (New York: Little Brown, 2002).
4. Derek Sivers, "How to Start a Movement," posted April 2010, www.ted.com/talks/derek_sivers_how_to_start_a_movement.html, accessed May 30, 2012.
5. See Merriam-Webster for the more modern definition of an Evangelist: www.merriam-webster.com/dictionary/evangelist, accessed May 30, 2012.

CHAPTER 5

Driving for Success

I skate to where the puck is going to be, not where it has been.

Wayne Gretzky, Canadian ice hockey player

GET ALL STAKEHOLDERS INVOLVED EARLY

A social media platform provides especially high value if it is used organization-wide—if really *everyone* in the organization can participate. That doesn't mean that all will and must. There will be a certain number of people who will provide content (often not more than a small percent of the total staff), and others who will read content or follow discussions. The goal should be to have diversity and to get ideas and input from all departments and corners of the organization, even if only a subset in each of those corners participates.

Different parts of the organization (different divisions, functions, or geographic units) will have a different view of what the enterprise social media (ESN) platform should provide them with, and some will still be not convinced it is a good thing in the first place. There will be fears of losing control, of distraction from "real work," and many other reasons why introducing something like an "internal Facebook" may be a bad idea. I will be discussing some of those fears in Chapter 6.

So what is the best way to get a successful platform running in spite of different positions? One important element of preparation is to start with a requirements-gathering phase that involves representatives from every part of the organization that might have a stake in an ESN. Requirements-gathering is a very important phase, but it often gets pushed aside or done incompletely, as there might be a preconception of what the solution looks like and people might become anxious to get to a product-evaluation phase instead, especially the more technically oriented stakeholders. But how can you make a good decision if the requirements of *all* stakeholders are not at least heard and discussed?

In the requirements-gathering phase, which is coordinated by the project manager, each of the stakeholders needs to ask some of the following questions:

- What do I want to get out of it—personally and for the group of people that I represent?
- What are some features that I think it should definitely have?
- What are some business rules I want it to support?
- What are some processes I would like to see changing based on the availability of an ESN?
- What are the best possible outcomes the introduction might have for my group, the organization at large, and me, personally?
- What concerns do I want to see handled immediately versus at a later stage?
- What integration capabilities will the ESN need to have with regards to other systems or initiatives that I might have a stake in?

These are some of the key questions, and the answers will result in some of the requirements that stakeholders have. The requirements need to be collected in a first phase and in multiple iterations through prioritization and a clear voting process. It is important to come up with a basic agreement on what the most important requirements are. In the discussion, it is important that people see the bigger picture and not only their own positions. In general, it is better to start with fewer features and complexity than to overload a system. While features like the various integrations with other systems are very important, some of them might be fairly complicated, and the trick is to find a good balance between a timely launch and satisfied stakeholders.

As the social network is going to be a new way of communicating, it should not be seen as another repository for documents—its value is based on dynamic growth and wide participation. So simplicity and ease of use should be at the top of the requirements list. Focusing on niche requirements that are of interest to only one group could hurt that simplicity. One exception to this might be legal requirements. Those, of course, might not be optional.

This phase of requirements-gathering serves purposes other than just defining what the new platform should look like and how it should behave. As stakeholders participate in this early stage, start a detailed thinking process to keep track of what they would like to see. Play with external social media networks, explore social media tools elsewhere and talk to friends or former colleagues about how they handle similar issues at their organization. They might look at Facebook with a new eye and try to identify features that they think are must-haves for an ESN and those that they really could do without (like advertising and certain games). So the stakeholders get more and more into the topic as a whole, they build some knowledge, and that equips them for better discussions.

The fact that they are asked to participate and have the chance to shape the final outcome in itself builds momentum, which will not only give you better buy-in early-on but also might build a great base of evangelizers that you will need at launch time. Of course, there will be those who might be somewhat disappointed when their proposed requirements do not make it to the final short list of initial key requirements. To keep this issue from disengaging stakeholders, it is important to communicate well within the group, and the project manager should make it clear that just because a requirement might not be handled in the very first phase of the project, it can still be on the table for a later phase. After requirements are collected, the group (or a subgroup of the complete team) will move into looking at actual solutions. Apart from functionality and the potential to handle business requirements, cost will play a key role at this point. This will again change what requirements will be covered by the solution and which ones will not. Some of the ones deemed less important might now come free with the chosen solution, while others deemed really important could actually be out of scope as solutions that provide them are just too expensive or take too long to implement.

In summary, getting all stakeholders involved early and getting their input to shape the solution is a key success factor and a careful requirements phase cannot be overestimated.

GO VIRAL

At SAS we had some early adopters spreading the news on the platform really quickly, which then lead to our social media platform going viral (see Exhibit 5.1).

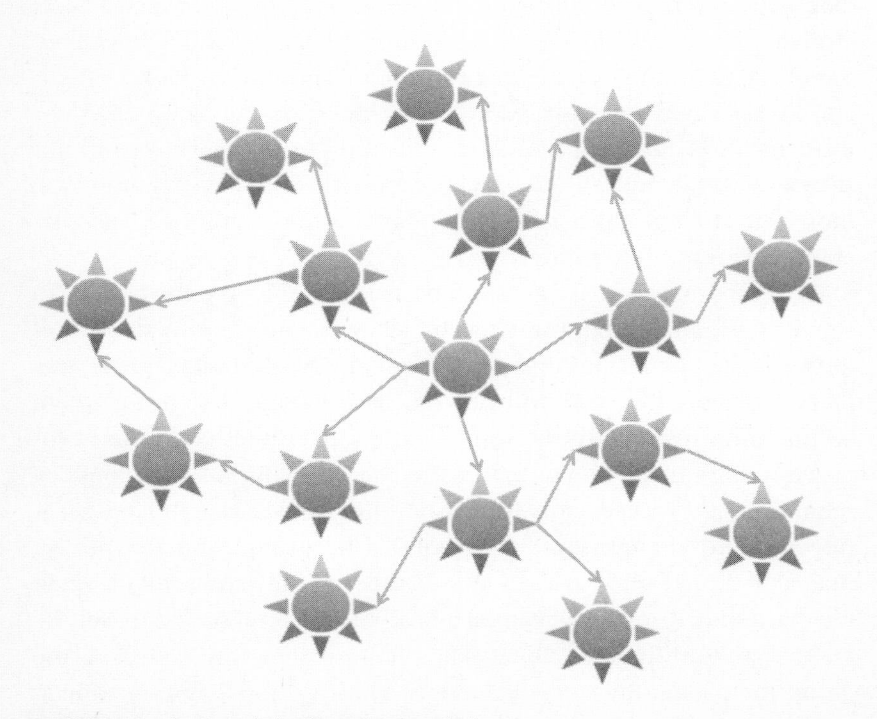

Exhibit 5.1 The Snowball Effect of Going Viral

One of the key features of social networks is some type of connection, either one-directional or bi-directional. On Facebook it is called "friendship," on LinkedIn it is called "connection," and on Twitter it is called "following." Those relationships are what weaves the network. Let's take an example from Twitter, one of the networks known for being the backbone of many viral incidents. If I have 600 Twitter followers and I send out a tweet (a short 140-character message), those 600 will be able to read it. How many of my followers will actually read the tweet depends on how many people they follow, how often they check their Twitter streams, and what their key interests are. But let's say for the example that my tweet is very interesting for a large portion of my followers and 200 of them do actually read it. One of the easy features of Twitter is retweeting, which means you take a message and repost it to your followers. So, of the 200 there might be 50 that find it interesting enough to do that. If any of those 50 have followers—and some of them might be very popular and have thousands of followers—my message could be retweeted exponentially. This means that thousands of people could see and read it, all within a matter of minutes or hours. If a message is very well prepared and tells an extremely compelling story or a piece of news that many people want to read, it will reach a number of people multiple times. If the message is on a special topic, the spread might be confined to a specific community, but even there it can reach a high rate of penetration. Messages that are very general and still very interesting can reach millions of people in a matter of days or weeks.

One of the key elements of viral spread is that it is usually spread by those in a community rather than the original author of a piece of content. Good examples of videos that went viral are out on YouTube (e.g., certain music and humor videos). If you see a video that has a few million views, you know it must have reached that viral level. At some point, content spreads not only via the virtual world, but also through the real world. People ask one another, "Have you seen this great video? I will send you a link to it." The connection is made in the real world, even though the actual sharing happens on virtual channels.

If you want your social media platform to spread fast and wide, you can actually use some advertisements that you know will spread widely. In Chapter 4, I explained the important role of evangelizers.

To the degree that those are connected within the organization, they represent a network of follower relationships, as described in the previous examples. A key, apart from a compelling, interesting message, is to reach people multiple times and from several angles. If your boss, your desk-neighbor, and three of your favorite colleagues from other sites point you to the new platform and recommend that you check it out, the probability that you will actually do so quickly increases. If the company president also endorses it along the way, that doesn't usually hurt, either. But if that president's message were the only push, success is far less likely than if peers and trusted connections endorse it as well.

In an interesting study,[1] Jonah Berger and Katherine L. Milkman from the Wharton School at the University of Pennsylvania found that emotions play a key role in why content is further distributed. In general, they found that viral spread is partially driven by psychological arousal. Content that evokes high-level positive (e.g., awe) or negative (e.g., anger, anxiety) emotions is more likely to go viral. Specifically, positive content is more likely to be shared than negative content. Content that evokes low-arousal or deactivating emotions (e.g., sadness) is less likely to go viral. In their study of *New York Times* articles they found that the effect of positive emotion is clearly visible, even if other external drivers—like the positioning of the content and other factors like how interesting, surprising, or practically useful it is—are factored out.

If you want your social media platform to spread virally, there are some things to keep in mind. These tactics will not necessarily guarantee it will spread like a viral video, but they definitely increase the chances:

- Create a compelling, interesting message.
- Keep it positive, but don't try to sell it directly; rather, sell it with some good stories that are strong enough to go viral on their own.
- Create some emotions in those stories so that your audience will be able to connect on a deeper level and be motivated to share the content.

- Humor can help, but be completely aware that humor has cultural limitations and what might go across very well in one culture might even be seen as an insult in another.
- Position the message and content in a way that will interest people. This could be on your Intranet, in an executive webcast, or through a message spread by top evangelizers. In the best case, all of these would work in a concerted, unified approach.

One thing to keep in mind is the timing effect. It could well take longer than planned to reach the tipping point, so you will need some breathing space in this. Don't give up too early, and remember that a single attempt with any message is not usually enough. Even if your network is already taking off, it is not guaranteed to be an ongoing success, so it is important that you plan marketing as an ongoing task and not a one-off launch activity.

FREEDOM WITHIN BORDERS: THE POWER OF GUIDELINES

One of the big myths around ESNs is that some users will produce a lot of negative energy, and there will constantly be cases that you need to manage because someone says something that is politically incorrect or too critical, and spreads quickly. It might be dependent on the general culture, but in all the cases that I have seen, this fear has been overestimated. One reason it doesn't happen as much as some of the pessimists expect is that a certain type of self-policing happens on the network itself. Like most other things on a social network, users are organically building and respecting norms for communication, and this happens relatively quickly. Some of this will happen outside of the network itself. A colleague might remind another to be careful about saying certain things in a certain way, or a manager might remind one of her staff to stay on the constructive side with their comments. A lot of our norms are built by observing others, and many of those engaging actively have experience from other external platforms or have had the chance to observe the ESN's unspoken rules before posting or sharing content themselves.

Despite this, incidents where someone goes too far can and will happen. There is one important activity you should go through that can considerably reduce the chances of these types of problems: The creation and proper rollout of social media guidelines. This is a task you should have already done for external social media activity (if your organization allows it), and it is a very good idea to set a similar framework for internal ESN use, and communicate it as widely and as often as you can. Coming up with some good guidelines is not necessarily simple, but it does not have to be a yearlong project, either. Some organizations have actually shared their guidelines with others, so you might find some out on the web that you can use to get started. It is important, however, that you adapt the guidelines to your own organization based on how mature your users are regarding social media.

In general, you want to create a framework that is wide enough to enable a certain degree of freedom, but at the same time provides some sensible boundaries. Exhibit 5.2 symbolizes such a framework.

Don't look at it as cutting people's freedom—it is unlikely that people in an organization will ever have complete freedom. There are always some rules that make engagement easier, more effective, and legally safe. So, in designing the rules for social media, you can actually

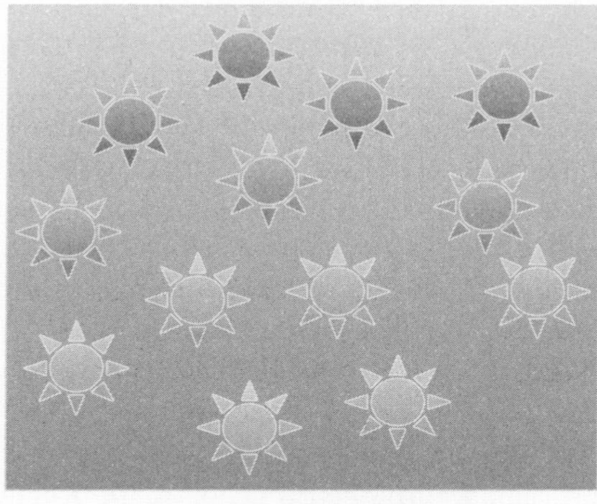

Exhibit 5.2 Freedom within Boundaries

draw from general rules. You don't need to start from scratch; you can start with the values and rules that govern and refine other interactions.

Typical rules need to cover:

- Business versus social content.
- Information to make clear that anything posted is open and might appear elsewhere within the organization.
- Rules about how to use pictures and what types of pictures are appropriate to use for profiles.
- Guidelines on how to comment on each other's content.
- Directions about the sharing of confidential information—even within an organization, there are limits as to what may be shared (e.g., some customer information tied to a project may not be shared even within one's own organization).

There are likely a number of other rules and guidelines that are more specific to your business, industry, or organizational culture. The key is that the guidelines are simple, clear, and well communicated. A good idea is to have people read and acknowledge them at the start of entering the platform. At SAS, we have people acknowledge them anew whenever they change. The acknowledgment step does not guarantee that everyone will read them, but it alerts users to the fact that there have been changes. More people are likely to actually read policy changes if they are presented in a short, concise manner.

Make sure to adapt the guidelines as needed. Behaviors that might need clarification often develop over time, and some of them need to be dealt with at the guideline level. While guidelines are supposed to provide a box within which people move freely, be prepared for certain users to push those boundaries. If a larger number of people begin to challenge those boundaries, try to understand why and consider adapting them.

TRAINING PORTFOLIO

As social media tools are usually quite straightforward to use, it is easy to think that training for an ESN is completely unnecessary. However, underestimating the need for proper training is one of the big traps that a team running such platform could fall into. While it is true that getting used to the features is usually a quick process—especially for basic functions like posting, liking, commenting, and connecting—those with minimal social media experience are likely to face a steeper learning curve. It is also easy to underestimate the need for business-oriented training. Users will need to learn how such a tool best fits into their business environment. Some of the key training topics that come to mind are:

- How to incorporate the platform into the portfolio of existing collaboration and communication tools.
- Guidelines and best practices on what to post where.
- Naming conventions for groups, tags, and titles.
- How to use notifications to balance being informed with getting overloaded.
- How to use the platform for different types of business problems.

Some users will figure out the answers to those questions by themselves, but many can really benefit from being introduced to some best practices as they become familiar with the platform.

Training can come in many different ways. A typical set of training methods is shown in Exhibit 5.3.

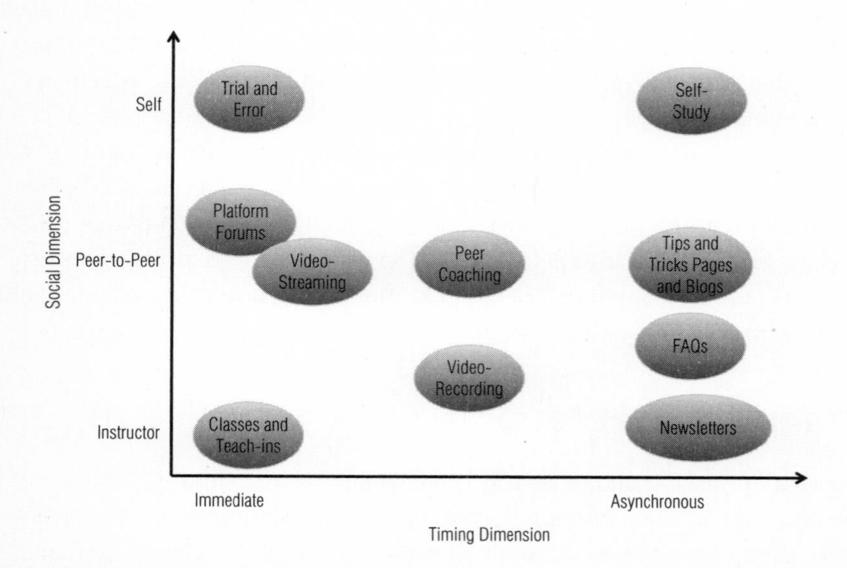

Exhibit 5.3 Training Portfolio

As the target audience for an ESN is basically the whole organization, training needs to be diverse. It is not enough to target technical people (or nontechnical ones), and the training portfolio should contain something for all levels of social media experience and technical predispositions. As people are rather busy, it can be difficult for them to attend training sessions; therefore, it is important to repeat the trainings and target a range of audiences. The ultimate goal is to reach a wide group of people, and not just the usual group that has an interest in the platform anyway.

Even for an ESN's regular users, it can take repeated reminders for proper use to become habitual. We have probably all experienced situations where we do not take something completely seriously until we have been exposed to it repeatedly. Reception can change depending on the format that information is presented in, the person presenting it, and the style in which it is prepared. At SAS, we had one of the top bloggers run a series of blog entries that introduced some of the tips for the platform in a very entertaining way. This is a format that might not be everyone's favorite, as some people prefer to get to the point right away, but it is very important to realize that your audience will be diverse and, in order to get the majority (getting everyone is not realistic at the beginning), you will need to have a portfolio of different options to reach them.

As people are often pressed for time to attend additional, full-blown training sessions, a series of regular small tips can be a great way to get people learning about some of the key features over time. At SAS we branded these as "Hub Tips" and ran them on a weekly basis. Tips should be archived so people can look at them anytime, but they should mainly be presented via small news items on the Intranet portal.

One group that can be very powerful evangelizers is that of executive managers. If they realize the ESN's potential and talk openly about it, it can really drive adoption up. A great way to reach executive managers is through short personalized demos that show off some of the positive collaborative examples that demonstrate some business benefit that will interest them. At the same time, show how easy it will be, even for them, to not only listen, but also participate.

The best way to plan the trainings is to make it part of your overall communication plan. The group best suited to plan that for you would be the internal communications team. It is highly recommended that this team be a part of your effort—in fact, they should be the core drivers, as they are very experienced in driving the message out.

That doesn't mean they should be the ones covering all those trainings. For strategies like self-study and peer-to-peer trainings, it is clear that others will be involved. Other elements can and should be delegated to a wider audience. Why not have an evangelizer in one of your line functions run a training specific to their group? This could ensure that acceptance within the training group is a lot higher. Another area where this makes sense is local language training. If the key language in your organization is English, for example, it would make a lot of sense to introduce your people to the platform in their own language. If you have a larger international organization, it is still a good idea to have your platform's interface language aligned (i.e., all in English), but still allow people to communicate with each other in their native language. Internationally spanning topic groups will benefit from agreeing on one language that is spoken by everyone.

As with many areas of an ESN, trying to control the audience is not a good idea—it sends the wrong signals and usually fails anyway. So, instead, work with some simple guidelines and let the rest develop on its own.

An ESN is driven by people's behavior and reactions, and therefore represents a complex environment. While it can never be fully controlled, it can be managed by providing a framework and having members adjust their behavior accordingly.

In summary, what is needed for success is a wide and diverse set of training opportunities and a set of guidelines that are simple enough to follow. Training needs to cover a lot more than just the technical how-to-use topics, and it should definitely cover business aspects and tips on how to best integrate the platform into the current portfolio of communication options.

Of course, people also enjoy those small tips that tell them how to get the best results. For Twitter there are tips on what to post, how, and when, to make sure the right audience reads it or responds to it.[2] Tips originally aimed at external social media are not in all cases fully applicable to internal social media platforms, but some can definitely help users become more effective and efficient.

PULSE

Knowledge flow initiatives need ongoing support, and one of the biggest mistakes a team launching a platform could make is to fire all their ammunition for the launch and forget to push very hard, on a very regular basis, for an ongoing time frame.

I refer to this type of pushing as "adding a pulse," and I think the analogy holds on several levels. What you really want is for your ESN to become a living entity, but just like every living species, it needs a pulse to survive, and it is not enough to pump a little blood in at the beginning and forget about it. The result will be a fairly quick and certain death.

An ESN rebirth can be just as hard as resuscitating a living organism. In fact, once something is declared dead, getting people to believe it can thrive again is rather hard (i.e., letting go of the pulse is very dangerous).

How should you go about keeping that pulse, though? The best way is a combination of news items, training activities, and special events. Here are a few examples for that last category:

- An Innovation Day, where you encourage all platform members or a specific subset of users to come up with ideas (either within a given framework or just free-form brainstorming).
- Connect the ESN to any possible event that is happening within your organization, be it on a regular basis or as a one-off. Have discussions with special tags for executive briefings or webcasts. Have one or more special evangelizers post live from external or internal events the company is involved in. This will draw a wider audience to the platform.

It is important to have a combination of those spreading out in a fairly regular pattern so it really forms a pulse and not only a few small spikes.

In Chapter 3, I talked about brand building. Apart from key events to get started, a pulse is necessary to establish a brand for the long term. You can see how the brand is becoming embedded in the community through how people talk about it—for example, how the platform name is used. At SAS, the name The Hub has quickly became a verb, as in, "I think you should hub that." So what you should develop is a theme that goes with the brand.

At Humana they call their platform Buzz, and those engaging on it are Buzzers. They even took the analogy to the point where people run around in Bee costumes for Buzz-related occasions. This might be going a little far in some cultures (remember to always be culturally aware and careful with certain activities if your platform is multinational or encompasses a diversity of cultures). The point is to create a brand, and embed it through ongoing pulse-like actions.

A pulse can also be created by individuals themselves. Most ESNs have notification capabilities that let you determine how often and in what form you would like to be updated or reminded to contribute. One good way of keeping notifications to a sensible level is to use a daily or weekly digest. This will create a regular event that reiterates that there is new and interesting content within areas the user defines, including questions waiting to be answered (potentially by them), updates from your contacts, and more.

One person who can drive the pulse regularly is the community manager. It will not be as automatic as reminders sent by the system, but it also has a personal touch to it. For instance, a CM could pull questions that haven't been answered for a while to the front of the platform or the home stream to make sure they get more visibility. Similarly, she could highlight certain controversial posts or give executive posts a special mention. In general, a regular post by an executive is another very powerful element to add to the pulse.

Another great way that The Hub at SAS is used for regular engagement is to send people specific thank-you notes. There can be a predefined set of occasions that could call for a thank-you note. Some examples:

- Thank you for good communication.
- Thank you for being a role model.
- Thank you for your mentorship.
- Thank you for being a visionary.

The plan is to enable administrators or community leaders to add additional thank-you categories that are more specific to the business activities. The nice thing about this feature is that you can use it to thank someone via the platform for something that might have happened actually completely outside of the platform. At SAS, not everyone is using the feature, but those that make it a habit end up guiding more people to the platform or thank-you note function. You can see the number and type of thank-you notes that someone has received over time. This is a nice way to give recognition and help build the pulse at the same time.

EXECUTIVE PARTICIPATION: NOT JUST BUY-IN

Introducing a social media platform is likely to impact a large part of the organization, especially if it is really planned and executed as an enterprise social media platform. Social media lives from scaling and wide distribution, so do not plan it for a niche of your organization. The most powerful ESN efforts aim to include the majority of the people. Even if not everyone participates in the end, targeting them all is a good way to reach the diversity and breadth of ideas that you are after.

If something is to influence the whole organization, it seems clear that you will need a certain level of buy-in and consent from your executive leadership team; however, it is more than just buy-in that is needed. If such a system is for *every* employee, it should also be for the executives, and this presents a chance to bridge a few gaps between executives and frontline employees. Communication between different levels can be difficult sometimes, and to overcome a we-versus-them feeling, there needs to be ongoing communication. So beyond buy-in ("I see the sense in creating something like this for employees to better communicate, exchange ideas, and share knowledge") you also need participation ("I want a platform that literally every employee, including myself and my executive management team, will use to communicate better").

Buy-in is the minimal requirement that you will need to launch the platform at an organization-wide level. Some of those platforms can be started relatively cost-effectively. The main reason that makes executive buy-in so important is not necessarily the technical investment. Even more important are investments like the following:

- Ongoing investment into resources running the platform and strategically developing it.
- Trust in opening up the organization for more transparency and open communication across levels and divisions.
- Buy-in at a certain level of cultural change that will need to happen for success—this might be induced by the platform itself.
- Letting go of some control and moving to different management styles.

The cultural change might actually be bigger than anticipated and, from the start, executives need to understand that an ESN might change the communication structures from top-down to more direct. On the one hand, this can lead to certain fears of losing control over what is happening in an organization. On the other hand, the fact is that a lot of that type of communication will happen anyway, though maybe not with the same intensity. In many organizations, control is likely to shift in any case these days, partly due to a lack of talent in certain key functions, but also because of an increased flexibility of the younger workforce that gives them power-by-foot, allowing them to leave the organization very quickly. Holding on to old power-structures will not be accepted by many of those young high-performers. With a rising number of knowledge workers, the old power structures are not likely to work long term.

The advantage of a social media platform where employees can discuss and communicate more freely is transparency. Many of the watercooler discussions will move to the platform, and even if employees remain less open than when talking in the hallway, much of the content will be indicative of what people feel is important and what is on their minds. How open ESN communication will really be depends on the existing culture, and there is often a learning and development process to increase openness.

Time will tell if those in control really mean it when they say they want a culture of open communication. The type and voice of comments will make all the difference. It is important that the leadership be very careful, holding back as much as possible when it comes to negativity or comments that can be viewed as being critical, especially in the early phase of the platform.

While negative comments from the leadership team should really be kept down, neutral and positive comments and personal posts are more than encouraged, and can actually have a greatly positive effect at the beginning. It could start with just general announcements that are written personally instead of being published in the form of very formal news items. Other very good examples of executive content include encouragement, true excitement about an internal or external event, or just a comment on something of relevance can have a positive driver effect for the social media platform and participation. In contrast, any activity by executives that even remotely smells like censorship or too much moderation can endanger the whole effort.[3]

It is important that this type of executive participation, while possibly encouraged and guided by communication specialists, remains a personal activity. A series of ghostwritten posts will be spotted by the community and will have different effects. At worst, they could make the we-versus-them culture even stronger; at best, they send the message that the platform is just tolerated by management, but toleration is not enough to harvest all possible benefits from your ESN initiative.

Many executives might be very careful with posting on the platform. The key is to give them some guidance. Just as they might have people help them address their employees in speeches and other messages, it would be helpful to have a communications specialist to get them started. Like with a lot of things, the first step is often the hardest. This is especially true with social media. The feedback, the interactivity, the value of comments—the effects of those are often underestimated, or at least misjudged at first.

Once it becomes a natural step in their daily routine to post to the platform and use it as one of their channels, it is often surprising how quickly executives see the potential, and some of them become real fans and frequent users.

Cultural change is often slow, so if an organizational culture is very hierarchical the process of opening up communication by using an ESN could take some time and, assuming that the executive team really wants more openness, they should take a careful approach in that case—especially with transferring some traditional hierarchical behavior into the platform.

Participation is the key to any social media platform and participation of the senior management team can be especially important, as it sends a number of key messages like:

- This is for everybody, including the boardroom.
- Open communication is wanted in this organization. We want *everyone* (including ourselves) to learn from anyone in the organization.
- Participation is easy—if a busy executive can do it, you can, too.
- We realize that knowledge lies in all pockets of the organization, and your knowledge counts even if you are not a senior employee, an acknowledged expert (yet), or working in the head office.

One of the key drivers for success is to work with executives so they become part of the community and don't just play the role of a sponsor.

NOTES

1. Jonah Berge and Katherine L. Milkman, "Social Transmission, Emotion, and the Virality of Online Content," http://opim.wharton.upenn.edu/~kmilkman/Virality.pdf, accessed May 30, 2012.
2. See the following HubSpot blog entry by Magdalena Georgieva on "5 Commonly Held Social Media Myths," http://blog.hubspot.com/blog/tabid/6307/bid/23478/5-Commonly-Held-Social-Media-Myths-Busted.aspx, accessed May 30, 2012.
3. See also comments from a Booz-Allen blog, "KM on a Dollar a Day," about why you shouldn't monitor or censor content and groups on social media platforms, accessed May 30, 2012.

CHAPTER 6

Fighting Barriers

Perfection is achieved, not when there is nothing more to add, but when there is nothing left to take away.

Antoine de Saint-Exupéry (1900–1944), French writer

FEAR OF LOSING CONTROL

Since I wrote my book on knowledge flow management (KFM) in 2010, I have found that looking at a KFM initiative from the perspective of the barriers turns out to present a good angle for making progress. It is based on the flow analogy and, as humans decide very often whether or not they want to share, working on barriers that hinder a natural flow seems to be a good way of getting started. I found in my courses and presentations that people can relate much easier to the barriers, and almost anyone can add something to the discussion. Looking at how to reduce those barriers with easy pragmatic approaches gives people a way to get started quickly, no matter where they are located in the organization. I've found that there is usually some barrier that every person can influence, so, in this chapter, I take that same approach and look at some common barriers that might be in the way of creating a successful enterprise social network (ESN) and making it work over time.

One of the big fears in connection to social media in organizations—sometimes openly expressed and sometimes present only as a hidden agenda point—is that of losing control. To a certain point, it is clear that allowing and enabling those in your organization to communicate completely freely with each other across some of the established organizational boundaries, without the consent and involvement of management, presents a new control structure. The question is to what extent did such control actually exist—often it is just wishful thinking that managers have that type of control. Passing some control openly and officially to employees is a strategy to get their commitment and involvement, an aspect that many organizational leaders have identified as a success factor. Without an engaged workforce, you cannot compete and innovate, and both activities are paramount to organizational success these days.

Another question one might ask is about the motives of control. Why and what do you want to control? Is it action? Is it behavior? Is it compliance? Organizations have always been complex, but the complexity has increased and so has the speed at which an organization must act and react to changing environments. The type of control that some have in mind is not possible anymore, anyway. Those days are over. To deal with complexity, it takes a good framework in which members of an organization may operate, but if decisions need to be made quickly and flexibly, control structures tend to slow down the processes that lead to those decisions. So loosening of control is something we need to design into our organizations to adapt to changing times.

An ESN is actually a very good way of loosening control. At the very least, it makes a lot of what is happening and evolving visible, to a certain degree. So we are not talking about giving up control and turning to complete chaos, but rather giving up managerial control to enable visible employee engagement.

Control is a strong cultural element, so if demand and control is still the guiding principle of your organization, it might be necessary to work on that element and see if there aren't areas where less control, more guidelines, and more involvement of all employees will help you make turns in your cultural development to help with organizational sustainability.

Interestingly enough, as real as this fear is, in some regards, the loss of control does not lead to complete chaos because managerial control is partly replaced by peer pressure and peer control. Those who post content or comments that go against organizational interests will usually be pointed in the right direction by those around them. I have seen this effect over and over with internal social media initiatives. This is not to say there aren't cases that might need management intervention, but the degree to which those incidents happen is largely overestimated. Unfortunately, the potential of their occurrence is often used as an argument against introducing social media.

The decision to introduce a social media platform should be based on a risk analysis that also includes the risk of losing out on potential communication benefits (learning, knowledge sharing, etc.) if a platform is not introduced. The risks need to be managed and they also need to be put into perspective. For some organizations, the decision could be to not introduce an ESN, or at least go forward only with some more restrictive rules and guidelines.

When you look at the types of organizations that are opening up to social media these days (e.g., military organizations, intelligence agencies, regulatory consultants, the press, and banks), you must wonder if your organization is really so different. Are the risks of opening up really more serious than in those cases, or is it just a matter of managing these risks and investing in proper resources driving the initiative?

It is hard to argue directly against fear—it just doesn't work to tell people to ignore their fears. These are often rooted in missing trust, as blogger Leslie White pointed out.[1] Diving in with some faith and dealing with issues in a trusting but guided way seems to be the best method to deal with some of those fears.

Even with all those arguments in favor of an ESN, it might not be for everyone. Collaboration can have its downsides. In some cases, it can produce groupthink, and when the culture is not aligned across an organization, it can create negative spirals. Other issues that can and often will occur include the spreading of incorrect information and a certain amount of information overload. But the benefits usually outweigh those downsides. So keeping them on the forefront of a decision to go ahead with an ESN is often just an excuse for managers who do not want to take that faithful jump into it.

If your organization's management is not ready for an ESN, it might need more time. In that situation, it is a good idea to launch and support some grassroots movements. They are almost guaranteed to appeal to some of the members in your organization, and their success will spread the word of value and finally reach the top, eventually having a chance to influence strategic direction. Those organizations that push back too hard will lose their smartest knowledge workers, as those increasingly expect this type of communication facility.

UNLEARNING

One of the barriers that hinders flows of knowledge is prior knowledge and how deeply it is embedded into people's thinking and behavior. It is best characterized by statements like the following:

- "But we have always done it that way."
- "This will not work here."
- "I know that this is the only way it will work."

Some of those can be explained by not-invented-here (NIH) syndrome. If I haven't been behind it, how can it be any good? Those types of statements reflect a certain type of attitude based on the urge to invent. Many people, especially technical experts, often think something is only of value if you developed it from start to end. Apart from the fact that this is almost impossible, as there is usually always something that you build upon, the notion of that being the honorable way can be difficult to get out of people's head—even if you explain to them that the most valuable inventions were not created in isolation, but by smartly connecting the dots.

It is hard to change those types of attitudes. To accept new ways of thinking requires a certain amount of unlearning. This does not mean forgetting, but rather accepting that a certain piece of knowledge that we acquired or learned might not be as firm and accurate as we assumed. Surrounding facts and contexts change, new information is added to the picture, and that means those things we learned will need to be questioned. So, I would see unlearning as the process that happens when we reduce the firmness of our assumptions and open ourselves to questioning and scrutiny, therefore letting information and interpretations into the picture that might completely overturn what we had learned in the past. If the distance between the prior knowledge and what might emerge from the new situation is especially large, this presents a hurdle, and one that can be hard to overcome. However, for people to advance and develop innovative thoughts this process is a prerequisite, as old paradigms and thinking structures prevent us from moving to new thinking.

When it comes to social media, one area where unlearning might have to happen is in the way that communication tools are structured, how they are used, and to what degree control is a driving element. In many cases, employees that start using a platform like this already understand the concept of email, but email is clearly very different from social media tools. Starting to use social media with a strong email-based approach might lead to people trying to digest content in the ESN as exhaustively and completely as they do with their email inbox. This level of interaction is not sustainable in a social media platform—at least not without sacrificing sanity. So what is needed is unlearning the email way and shifting towards the social media experience. The keyword in that last sentence is *experience*. It is very hard to explain to people the differences between social media and email communication; it is usually easier for people to grasp by just starting to use it. By trying it out with a fairly open mind, one is a lot more likely to experience the difference and get the hang of it more quickly.

Unlearning is not only necessary for the acceptance of the platform itself, but also concerning the discussions that go on in the platform. As I pointed out, innovation and learning is supported by an impulse for change. The involvement within an ESN exposes people to a range of opinions, and usually those are presented by not only a single individual, but also confirmed or expanded on by peers of the original presenter (e.g., through likes and comments). A group is often stronger and more convincing than an individual when outlining a new line of thinking, and hesitant users might think, "Well, if everybody thinks that way, maybe I am wrong and should question my assumption." Therefore, a diverse global community, as represented by social media, has more chances of setting certain trigger points for unlearning. Of course, the reverse can also be true in some cases, where a certain group just confirms what they believe and stagnant groupthink is the result. To repeat: The larger, more diverse, and more independent a group is, the better the chances that unlearning can happen.

DEALING WITH "STUPID"

One barrier for the early phases of an ESN is the belief of a number of organizational members who think they can be a good judge of what questions, posts, or comments might be "bad" and which ones might be "good." If you have people in your organization that feel that way and are in a powerful position, they can really drag your platform down and stifle any type of open conversation.

Very often when people talk about "stupid questions" they see it from their own position, state of mind, or experience; but from the perspective of the person asking the question, the world might look quite different. Let's take the example of asking the same question more than once. While the person judging the question quality might think it has been asked and answered many times before, there might be a range of reasons why the asker has never seen an answer, let alone the question in the first place. Another quality element of a question is sophistication. What might be a really easy or even seemingly irrelevant question to one person might be very important and central for someone else.

One advantage of an ESN is the broad direction of many questions, which is slightly different than that seen in mailing lists, where there is more of a defined audience. An ESN's wide audience represents different levels of sophistication, and chances are that an answer will come not from the super-expert who deems the question "stupid," but from a person who just recently found the answer, or someone who often deals with questions at that level (a trainer, for example).

One of the characteristics of social media platforms is that there will be no way that any individual can digest all of the posted content. This is one of the things that users will have to learn if they come into the platform with an email mindset. A "stupid" question might actually not even be noticed by everyone, but the social platform could magnify two effects:

1. When the question is being asked in a group or subcommunity, it could reach people who do, in fact, deem the question too basic.
2. When a question is asked in more general post streams, it could very well reach a wide audience and increase the chance that someone with the right mind-set and experience will answer it.

But even in the first case, by being active in other groups and discussions in the platform, even experts in one topic are likely to be part of a community where they are new to a topic and could be asking basic questions in the eyes of experts in that community.

It is this type of acceptance that is needed to build the necessary trust for people to ask a range of level of questions and a wider range of people make progress on topics by listening into the conversation.

Social media platforms can always form specific groups for topics and even make them private or by-invitation-only if users are concerned that their discussion will be watered down by too many non-experts. This is a valid approach and is one of the reasons why mature ESNs often have a growing number of private groups.

If there are a lot of questions that are deemed too basic and this becomes more obvious when a social media platform surfaces, this could actually be valuable to know by the organization as it could indicate that:

- The level of expertise might be lower than believed.
- There are deficiencies in the training material and how people are reached.
- Documentation is not sufficient or not easy enough to find.
- Corporate and marketing messages are not reaching people.

To investigate such issues, interested parties can scan discussions and questions using a predefined search tool or keywords. Instead of blaming an individual for asking such a low-level question, it is worthwhile to investigate if there isn't a bigger problem.

In summary, there might still be "stupid questions" in the eyes of certain experts, but an ESN makes it more likely that there will be some people out there who can put themselves into the shoes of those asking and put the best effort into answering properly with the right language.

INTEGRATION

When a new ESN channel is introduced, it will never be on a clean slate where no other communication channels existed before. At a minimum, people will have had face-to-face communication, but it is actually a lot more likely, especially in larger organizations, that an individual has a whole list of channels to choose from (e.g., email, content management systems, instant messaging, a corporate newsletter). As a result, people will not necessarily be happy to get another channel to use and manage. This is especially true if the team introducing the ESN does not succeed in making a good case for why the new channel has advantages and how it fits into the overall channel portfolio. Such weak communication can present a barrier to usage for many potential users. One frequent argument in this discussion is the fact that the channels are not well integrated. Depending on the existing infrastructure and the number of existing channels, integration can be a big challenge. Often people have really high expectations as to integration, however. They state that they want everything in once place through one channel. The effort to create such a one-stop-shopping portal can be quite an expensive endeavor, and the question remains if it is really possible to create such a portal or if it isn't more of a pipe dream. Especially if people do not want to spend the time to customize portals, it will be very hard to anticipate the different needs of different users at different levels of expertise.

As a result, it is often more pragmatic to accept the fact that there will be multiple channels and look at smart integration possibilities. In today's world it is unrealistic that all the information flowing toward us comes in a single channel and, as the interaction between organizations become increasingly more dynamic, the same is true within an organization. We can strive for a reduction, but expecting a one-channel life is like joining the Amish.

The fact is that with a rising number of channels, life gets more complicated as we need to manage what is flowing at us and this represents a barrier for people to engage in yet another platform.

Therefore, it is important to tackle this issue and not ignore it. In my mind, there are two approaches for fighting this barrier:

1. Education on how to best manage multiple channels and how to decide which to use for the task at hand.
2. Integration of channels and systems, where possible.

Education can range from lists that explain channels and their typical usage to full business training via all the different methods explained in Chapter 5 in the section entitled, "Training Portfolio."

Integration can happen at a number of different levels. At the system level, it can really unite source systems and represent them as one. This is sometimes possible, but it also means adaptation of the primary channels to that system and retraining some of the users. At the interface level, it might result in a portal approach, which presents it own challenges, as I discussed earlier in this chapter.

A very good way of integrating when it comes to social media platforms is to integrate just the collaboration features of the platform into other channels. Here are a few examples:

- Have comments on the Intranet news area fully integrated with the ESN (i.e., any comment on the news item is visible in the platform and integrated into a person's posting stream). Also, people can use the like feature directly from the news item and see the number of likes it has received so far. These are two integrations that bring content and discussion together closely (see Exhibit 6.1).
- Integrate web-based and other collaboration tools, like discussion streams integrated into communities on Microsoft SharePoint team sites (see Exhibit 6.2).
- Host webcasts (from another channel) alongside discussion streams that are directly integrated into the webcast interface (see Exhibit 6.3).

As a result of any of these integrations, users do not need to get involved in more than one system/channel to read or post information. Instead of launching the platform while watching the webcast, they can just type into the webcast interface and comments will also be visible to those following a given tag on the platform during and after the event as well.

Those types of integration do not change the individual channels (and for some more directed and targeted information-gathering this can actually be an advantage) and they also offer the possibility

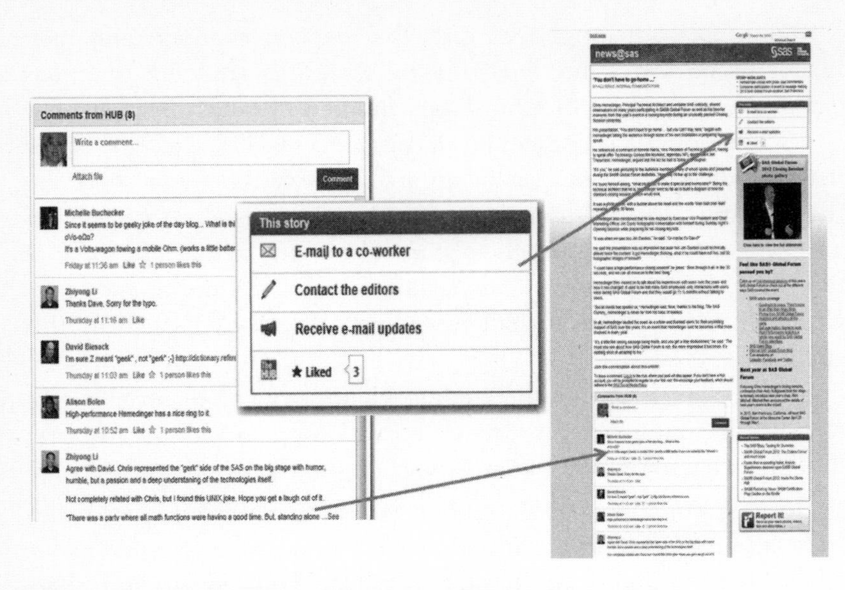

Exhibit 6.1 The Hub—Newsletter Integration *Source: © SAS*

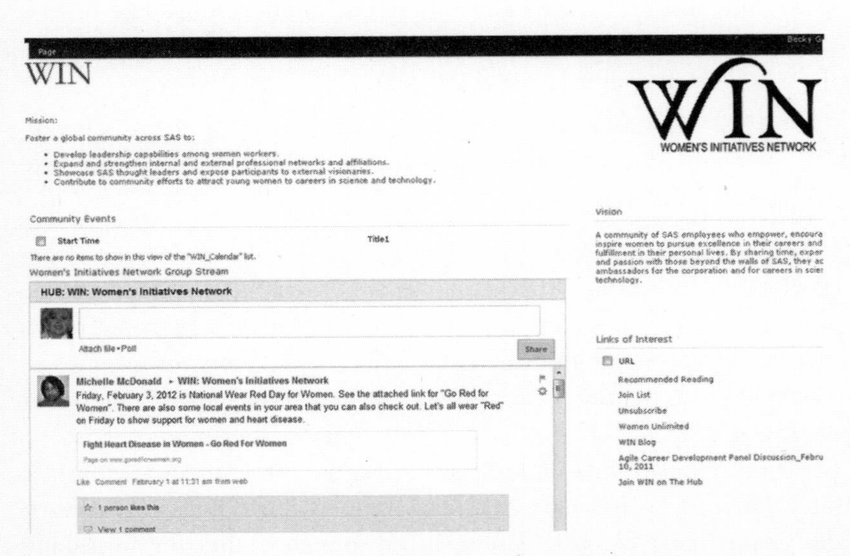

Exhibit 6.2 The Hub—Microsoft SharePoint Integration *Source: © SAS*

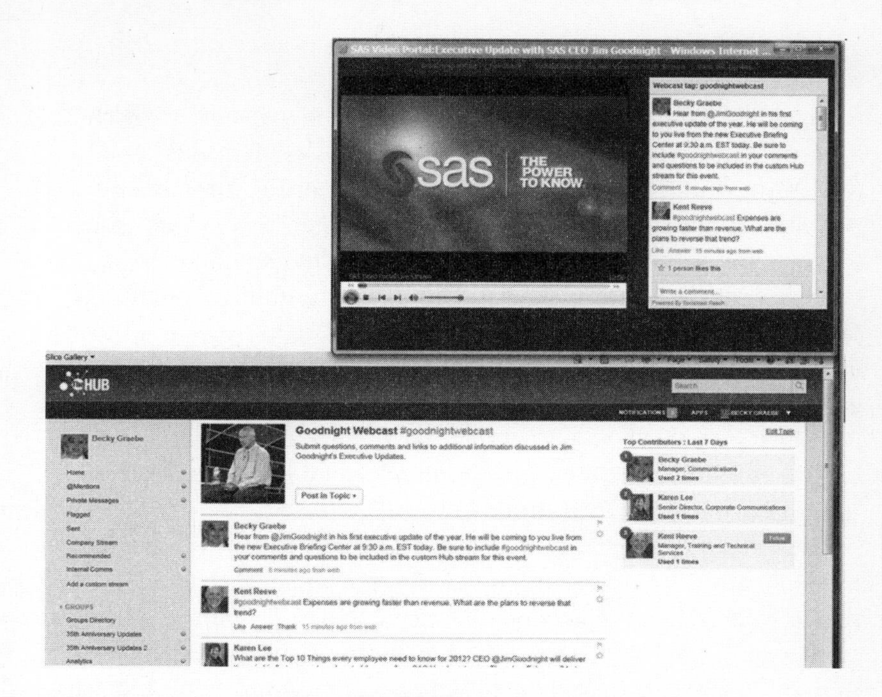

Exhibit 6.3 The Hub—Webcast Integration *Source:* © *SAS*

to act in both worlds—the original channel and the social media platform—at the same time. This is somewhat different than a triggered move of messages—for example, a connection between external social media platforms like LinkedIn and Twitter, where a post on Twitter automatically also gets posted on LinkedIn. Those integrations can be useful as well, but they do not fully integrate the discussion as they are mostly one-directional. The multi-direction examples listed above, are more about embedding the discussion into another interface, where it can be viewed and discussed by a wider range of users.

Another benefit of those type of integrations is that, after a while, users will realize that their discussions are happening in more than one place, so it will be less of a hurdle—and even an encouragement—to go to the other channel and continue the discussion there, with the potential benefit of getting them to experience the new channel's unique advantages.

An important integration area is that of source data, including personal data or pictures. As there will be traditional data sources for personal data (your HR systems mostly), the question is whether it is possible to connect this database with the social media platform. The fields from the HR system that should make it into the platform are probably limited to name, position, manager, and other general information of the type as it is usually visible to all employees via the company directory (if you have that as an online system). It is important that those are consistent across systems. Users do not want to hunt for the correct information after finding differences—for example, the spelling of a name—across systems. The information fields in the ESN will be easily visible by anyone, including oneself. The fact that users can see their own listed information also makes it easier to spot errors and correct mistakes.

Another area that needs good integration is that of profile pictures. Pictures are a very important feature in a social network, and that includes those that people share to make a point or a deeper connection with colleagues. Profile pictures play a special role, though. Social networks aim to support communication, and while face-to-face communication would be ideal, a social network is a scaled-down way of communicating. It is missing a lot of sensory information that we get when we meet someone in person. Connection via video would cover at least a few more of the nonverbal communication cues that we miss and, as bandwidths increase, we will see an increasing usage of video connections for that matter, either directly in the ESN or through another channel (e.g., video chat via Microsoft Lync). Many times messages flow only as text, however, and that is where a profile picture adds important additional information. First of all, it offers immediate recognition for those users that I have dealt with in the past. For those I don't know from face-to-face meetings, at least I can build that recognition over time. There are people that are very uncomfortable with posting a picture and, although it cannot be made mandatory, it should definitely be encouraged that everyone have one. Here we should address the fact that the request to provide a picture profile alone can be a barrier for some people.

In case your organization already has applications that include pictures of people, you will need to think about a sensible integration. Examples of those prior systems are:

- An online staff directory.
- A SharePoint MySite implementation that lets people create a profile with a picture.
- A possibility to add pictures to the email registry (as in Microsoft Exchange).

As you now add another platform, you will need to decide if you want to allow a different picture provided for each system or integrate them all so that the same picture is displayed in all cases, meaning that if one gets updated, they all do. Some people will immediately complain about missing integration in this area, but before you jump in and spend a lot of effort trying to integrate pictures across every possible channel, consider alternate views as well.

It depends on the individual whether they might want to have different pictures in different places. One reason to prefer different pictures could be that each platform is used differently. As an example, I usually have a different profile picture on Facebook, which I use mostly for private purposes, than I have on LinkedIn, which is much more business-oriented. The same could be true within an organization, where users might want to have an official picture that stays constant—for example, in the staff directory—while the one in the ESN changes a lot more frequently and can be updated whenever a user wants.

A possible solution would be an interface that would allow people to decide whether they want their picture synchronized across or not. Such a feature would appeal very likely to the more technical people, but it could also add a level of complexity, and keeping it simple could mean different things for different levels of users. Some users would say it is simpler to have one picture across all platforms, while others would say it is simpler to choose which picture appears on each different channel.

In general, smart integration, if it makes things simpler, is something to strive for, as disintegration represents a barrier for a certain type of users you want to win over. Not all types of users will see this as a huge issue, however. Those who have extensive experience with external social media platforms will be used to hopping onto new channels, even if they are not integrated with those they had in the past. While these users would love to see some integration (it could be a selling argument for them as well), it usually doesn't keep them from trying out new platforms.

NO TIME TO POST: PORTFOLIO MANAGEMENT

One big barrier for many users who hesitate to participate in a social media platform (internal or external) is best expressed in the statement: "Sorry, but I do not have any time to post to another platform."

It is probably true that they are busy with many things and adding an extra activity does not seem possible, but one must understand that a social media platform can replace some other activities, and should not be seen as a completely new add-on to their channel portfolio. In many ways, it can save time when switching certain tasks from the original channel to the new one.

Here are some examples, where using an ESN can either save time or enhance chances to get a better answer, which raises quality:

- Instead of sending an email to one or more groups (and potentially wasting time for everyone who needs to open and read the email) post it to the social media platform, exposing it to a wide range of people and potentially getting a much faster answer.
- Instead of chatting in an isolated messaging program, start a discussion on the ESN and not only get a larger range of answers, but also come to a decision point faster, as more perspectives and arguments are more quickly presented.
- Instead of sending messages about events to a large audience in a mailing list, create a Twitter-like posting stream (a microblog), which those who are really interested can choose to follow, and those who are not interested can easily ignore.
- Instead of going through a lengthy editing process very quickly post a news item with a few words and a relevant link to highlight an event, article, or milestone on the spot.

- Instead of using many different channels to reach a fragmented audience, use the one social media platform to reach a larger audience with a single post, where you can get a more comprehensive discussion.

So the question should not be "Do I have the time to post?," but "Which is the best channel for me to post?"—and, often enough, the answer (especially when your platform is running successfully) will be "Via social media!"

LEGAL CONCERNS

Especially in recent years, with the growth of stored data and information, legal concerns around information sharing have grown as well. The right information in the right hands can have tremendous power—but the right information in the wrong hands can be equally powerful, and dangerous. As it becomes easier to get access to information, it also becomes more likely that those wanting to harm will find ways to get to the valuable information they want to exploit. It used to be that to steal trade secrets from an organization, you had to get hold of a piece of paper and maybe copy it (to ensure the theft was not noticed); but with digitization, you could now take millions of those pieces on a tiny little memory stick and walk out the door with it undetected. While there are special tracking systems available that can record that someone accessed particular data (people reviewing the logs were able to sense something malicious), such a theft would likely stay unnoticed, at least long enough for a person to do serious damage.

One way to make those incidents less likely is with some security processes including special passwords, encryption, and special access to certain buildings, computer rooms, and files. Very often the failing element in this security chain is not the technology; rather, a person authorized to access the data who, at some point, ceases to be loyal and takes advantage for personal benefit.

One recent example allowed the German government to buy a number of CDs with the data of German taxpayers with accounts at Swiss banks. The data was stolen by some bank employees and offered to the German government. As a result, many taxpayers were charged with tax fraud and many more turned themselves in. One would have thought that a Swiss bank would have rather strong security procedures to avoid that type of theft. Whether you are for or against this type of data sharing (the Swiss banking industry was, of course, less supportive than the German government, which recovered hundreds of millions of dollars), the fact is that the data was not supposed to leave the banks, but it easily did.

If a Swiss bank has issues holding onto sensitive data, it seems obvious that many other organizations will as well. Information leaving the organization is only one of the risks that the legal department (and the IT department, of course) is very concerned about. Information sharing usually leads to information usage, and there is a range of uses that are improper and could lead to legal issues. The following are just a few risky behaviors:

- Sharing information and details from customers or partners within the organization, even though there are limitations as to how far it is allowed to be shared (i.e., any type of classified material).
- Sharing information that is to be used only within an organization on external social media platforms or discussing it with external parties.
- Endangering trademarks by not properly using them.
- Infringement of copyright by sharing documents that are protected from such duplication.
- Usage of personal data across the organization.

Those are just a few examples, and the rules and regulations around some of those processes can become rather complicated. What makes it even harder is that there are different regulations in different countries.

When launching a social media platform you are by definition making it easier to share information within your organization. As such, you make it easier for the good causes, but you also make it easier for the bad ones. The big question is whether the risks are bigger than the opportunities, and how you can limit risks and make sure you have good processes in place to deal with potential incidents.

When looking at this you have to remember that very often people are your weakest link. In that sense, a social media platform is not so different from information storage you had before: Anyone with access to it represents a certain risk. Even with a social media platform, you will surely have other systems that contain classified and restricted information that is not accessible to everyone. The risk comes into play when people with access engage on the ESN platform, and share information that should not be shared. If you think about it, this can easily happen in any communication channel—private email, in-person conversations, and chats at the real-world watercooler.

Yes, it is easier to share information on a social media platform, but at the same time it is more transparent what gets shared (i.e., it happens more in the open where it is visible by peers, managers, and anyone else). So it is actually more likely to be detected than if it were to be shared through direct channels (unless a company monitors all chats and email—something that is not likely to raise trust with employees).

The fear that an ESN could largely increase the likelihood of any of these incidences is real and valid. The question is whether the problem is due to the platform or something else. Loyalty and responsibility are values that members of an organization need to embrace to reduce the chances of such incidents occurring. With a successful ESN, chances are that you have a higher trust level and better connection between your employees, making it potentially easier to catch any glitches or wrongdoings.

As mentioned, those legal rules, laws, and regulations can be rather complicated. Therefore, it is very important to engage your legal experts as early as possible into the whole process of launching an ESN; it would be rather dangerous to wait until any wrongdoing is noticed. If involved early, legal experts can actually help build some of the frameworks within which organizational members can operate efficiently. There is the danger that the involvement of a legal expert might slow things down to a certain extent, but this is a precaution that can actually save time and money in the long term.

There are actually more and more legal experts that are aware of the unique issues that ESNs present, and can make sure that business is affected minimally, while covering the legal requirements correctly.

The lesson to take away here is to work closely with your legal experts. They can actually make a lot of things easier for you as well. For example, they can help you design cultural and legally correct disclaimer notes and company policy documents.

NOTE

1. "Fear and Social Media" blog entry on Socialfish, www.socialfish.org/2011/08/fear-and-social-media.html, accessed May 30, 2012.

CHAPTER 7

Technology: The Enabler

People are inherently creative. They will use tools in ways the tool's makers never thought possible.

Steve Jobs (1955–2011), late Apple CEO

SOCIAL OR SUPPORTING SOCIAL

One of the reasons that social media has made it into organizations is, clearly, the growing usage of these types of tools and platforms on the web. People of all ages have experienced the effects that social media tools have had, and they continue to rely on them in their lives. While not all of it seems immediately transferable into daily business life, the potential benefits of interacting and sharing with others within an organization have become obvious to many. Part of this shift is based on the business models of social media platforms, which became very successful even though they offered the majority of their services for free. One way to cash in was to transfer what worked externally into organizations.

One example of a tool that has found tremendous success external to and within organizations is Google search. A number of organizations find it very appealing to have their internal content just as easily searchable as the rest of the external web. The result was the introduction of Google appliances—black-box machines that would be placed in organizations, index a broad range of content, and present a localized search interface that was a lot better than what prior search technologies could offer.

One of the reasons why such technologies are considered to be worth paying for is that they are proven to work. They have been developed and tuned for several years in a challenging environment where there are literally hundreds of millions of users and billions of pieces of content. Those are the conditions that make you develop something quite robust, which will not usually have any issues scaling within a typical organization.

Another reason it was not a big hurdle to get organizations to accept Google was the sheer fact that they were known. Users are familiar with the company's name, services, and reputation, all of which introduce an element of automatic trust. Because of the wide range of users they targeted, the intraorganizational technologies had remained simple or they would not have made it to the level of adoption they were able to reach. Apart from simplicity, a growing number of people are very familiar with platforms like LinkedIn, Xing, or Facebook. More and more people have at least some experience with the new concepts of tagging and following, as introduced by Twitter. Commenting and liking others' content and online behavior is something most people have done before–and some people do it many times a day.

The effects those social tools have had on our lives has become a growing topic in the media (traditional as well as digital) and has been the focus of numerous books and articles. Research and teaching turned to it as well. And in the business world, the dream to become the next Google or Facebook has become a driving force for many new startups.

Before I look at the effects of social media technology a little more closely, I want to start out with a short discussion on the word *social* in all of this. I will not use the term social technology, as that has a predefined meaning left over from the early twentieth century that might be a little too philosophical for our purposes here. Often when people think of technology in a social sense, it is more likely to mean the tools and platforms that we now use to socially interact. It is important to note, though, that the technology is only an enabler for those social interactions; it is a platform, a tool that will make it possible to have social interactions with others in spite of not being physically face to face. As a result, one should be very careful with the expectation that providing such a platform will be enough to drive those social interactions.

A lot of the growth of social media platforms started in the non-virtual world, with people telling each other about a platform (usually in real life) before engaging there. This usually happens on a smaller scale, but I would say it was a growth driver nevertheless. Examples include instances like real-world friends deciding to connect on LinkedIn, or new colleagues saying after a meeting, "I will friend you on Facebook." Since getting used to the Xing business network platform, I usually only keep people's business cards until we connect on Xing. I do this instead of keeping the business cards in a drawer, adding them to an address book or scanning them into a computer and logging the information on a database. However, there are additional elements to social media that make it so much more powerful. The fact that all users own and manage their own data is a key benefit. While the email or phone number on that business card in your drawer will eventually be out of date, the social media link will stay current, provided your contact updates the profile. An additional benefit to social media is that, through a link, so much more information is shared than can ever fit on a business card. You can even get to know another person to some degree through these channels, so you won't feel that you are starting from scratch when you eventually meet in person. If you still rely on business cards and static contact lists, some of the data you have is likely to be wrong. To update it, you might need to wait until you run into the person again, so you can ask for the latest and greatest at that time. With a social media platform like LinkedIn or Xing, you don't even have to ask anymore, a person's key pieces of information are at your fingertips, and they are always up-to-date.

Whether a technology itself is *social* as opposed to being a *social enabler* is determined by the amount of guidance you devote to helping the social interactions happen, especially in the early phases of an enterprise social network (ESN). The expectation that if you build it, they will come will often lead to disappointment, as I have experienced with other knowledge flow management initiatives. The failure of many knowledge management (KM) projects is likely due to this one misconception.

With the advent and the huge growth of social media platforms on the external web, people fall into the same trap again. Those launching a social media platform can be deceived by how easy it is to use from the technical side and, at the same time, underestimate the importance of the necessary human and social support structure. Many people who fell into the KM trap the first time around now think something like, "Well KM did not work before because the technology was too complicated; now that it is easier it will definitely work all by itself." Without taking the holistic view of knowledge flow management (KFM) that I propose, a social media KM venture will fail just as miserably as it did the last time around.

I WANT AN INTERNAL FACEBOOK

As discussed in the last section, the notion of what an ESN might look like is shaped by what people see externally. Often, the discussions start by using well-known external platforms as examples and talking about some of the differences. As a result, the one driving the technology side of it might say something like, "What I had in mind would be an internal Facebook within the firewall." On the one hand, that comparison is useful as it describes what type of platform one has in mind. On the other hand, if people don't like certain Facebook features or behaviors, the comparison could create misconceptions and anxiety. The way that Facebook has succeeded in taking up a larger and larger portion of people's time will surely spawn the idea that an ESN is a time-waster—an idea common with many senior leaders who do not understand the potential benefits. Similarly, among Facebook's fastest-growing features are apps, games, and advertisements, which are not necessarily associated with productivity in an organizational setting.

If you use the Facebook analogy to explain what an enterprise social media platform might look like, it is important that you point out some significant differences. Here are some examples:

- If you use advertising at all in your ESN it will be to highlight strategic initiatives and news that can help keep the site business-focused. Since advertising is a key component of Facebook's business model, it is designed to distract users from the task at hand and sell them something. This is not part of the model for an internal ESN.

- The user community of your ESN will be defined by organizational boundaries. On Facebook, while there are options to control who tries to contact you, it is nevertheless left up to an individual to set them appropriately. As a result, the number of people who potentially have some plans to annoy or harm other users is a lot higher on an external, independent platform. An organization can control its platform in regards to who can log on and who cannot, which makes it easier to control this type of behavior.
- While most Facebook statistics are only available to certain Facebook employees, your organization can have access to a range of useful measures that make it a lot easier to understand where the platform is moving to and what is actually happening.
- Externally, successful platforms like Facebook have a huge number of registered users. Despite this, only a subset actively uses it on a daily basis, and an even smaller subset actively contributes, but due to the large number of registered users, even a small subset can be millions of people. Such a platform likely represents a wider type of audience when it comes to age, skills, or cultural background. Your ESN will usually deal with smaller numbers in each of these categories. Smaller numbers might result in less diversity and less chance of a critical mass of engaged users to drive topics forward.
- A big part of making an ESN successful is a focus on good community management. A community should have a solid feeling of who is a part of the community and how the organizational culture might be driving their behavior and actions. This provides a better chance for more targeted involvement and encouragement. On the one hand, if that community manager is already well known and well respected, it could make it easier for him to be heard. On the other hand, if the

community manager is known for repeatedly failing to make knowledge management work, the strategy could also backfire.

- Security plays a different role in an external platform than it does in an internal one. An ESN is usually within the firewall of the organization, while an external platform is on the Internet. Actually, the growth of mobile access to internal resources can open additional security risks to even an internal platform; however, the biggest risks are usually the people themselves—just like on external networks. In many cases, security is one of the key reasons that organizations start creating an ESN initiative. They just do not feel it is safe for employees to discuss business information on external platforms, even those that might have access controls to limit use to their organization only. As long as information is hosted externally, the trust element plays an important role, and the legal department, IT, and management feel a lot better keeping it within the borders of the organization.

With all those differences, using "internal Facebook" is not likely to describe what you really want. But mention it as a very broad description of what a social media platform might look like can be better than trying to explain all the features in detail. The conversation starts with a very broad idea of what you are after; more detailed discussions can happen later.

THE POWER OF SIMPLICITY

The technology that drives an ESN can be put into a few categories:

- **The interface**: The most important element, as it gets people to the platform and keeps them coming back.
- **Groups and content categorization**: Those are the features that group either people or content in different ways. It extends into features like tagging or content stream management.
- **Security**: Most of what happens on an ESN is open, but there are some cases where security is still very important, especially regarding access to the network itself, and, even more so, access via mobile devices from outside the firewall.

- **Administrative interface**: An ESN needs to be managed so it is important that related tasks are easy and the key features are in place from the start. This is especially important because the number of support staff (be it technical or community management staff) is usually quite small. Sometimes one or two people for a platform hosting 20,000 users or more can be enough.
- **A good set of statistics**: These help steer the initiative and are an important part of the administrative interface.
- **An API (an application programming interface)**: It is important to have an API that allows for extension of the functionality, as needed. This flexibility is essential to make sure the platform will grow with the needs of the users and their maturity.
- **Integration capabilities**: Either through the API or via out-of-the-box functionality, it is important to offer integration capabilities. Unless the platform is really created on a technological greenfield (i.e., in a very small organization), there will always be prior systems and platforms that people already know and that will remain active even after the ESN comes along. A frequent candidate for integration is a collection of Microsoft SharePoint sites that are already being used for sharing. The integration is very important as it allows you to provide a more comprehensive view and also makes it easier for users to transition to the new platform. An example of integration is the ability to comment on news articles and other content that appears on the Intranet but is also accessible via the integrated ESN.

The importance of the first element in this list, the interface, cannot be stressed enough. Specifically, it is the simplicity that is so very important. One of the reasons certain platforms are so successful is that they are inherently limited in their functionality. Most often there are only three or four core functions that users need to familiarize themselves with: post, comment, like, and connect.

For years, computer interfaces were dominated by feature competitions. Driven by Microsoft, which had a tendency to give users any imaginable feature they might ever want and more, people became somewhat tired of trying to figure out where each feature was and what it did. One company that anticipated the shift to more clarity better than any other was Apple. Driven relentlessly by simplicity fan Steve Jobs, Apple moved towards interfaces that were simpler and offered a lot fewer features applicable to niche users only.

The idea of *less is more* is behind the success of many social media tools that follow the same strategy. In spite of this, many ESNs are being implemented by IT teams that have held onto the idea that *more features are better*. In these cases there is a big danger that they will ask for and implement more and more features, just because they think it would be cool to have that. Instead, I strongly recommend questioning the addition of any features, even those that users are asking for. In the old paradigm, if 5 percent were asking for a feature it was considered worthwhile to have; but if you are focusing on simplicity, you need to focus on the 95 percent for whom this feature is not of interest. Adding it might make things more complicated for them, even if it means that they have just one more menu item or one more screen element.

This is a paradigm shift, and it is important to not leave the decisions to only IT. Community managers, the communications department, and the knowledge management professionals within the strategy team need to make sure that feature creep does not take over.

Another way of making it easy for contributors is by offering access to the platform at anytime from anywhere. This is possible through mobile apps. Access to social networks via mobile devices is a big growth area, as it offers ways to share things in real time. This also makes it more likely that an incident is shared. It reminds me of an iPhone app I use to send postcards by taking a picture, typing a sentence, selecting an address from the address book, and hitting send—all within minutes. It was that immediacy that made me write postcards again (albeit in digital form). And the best part is that there is no need to hunt for stamps in some foreign place. Making it easy to post from anywhere removes a barrier to use. It is more likely that people will post if they can do so on the spot rather than having to move back to their desktop, for example.

Another small feature that can make an interface easier to use is the simple ability of allowing people to edit their posts (at least shortly after posting). This takes away fears of posting an embarrassing typo publicly and having no way to fix it. As a general rule though, the convention must be to change only the format (or error) and not the key message, especially if someone else has already commented on it.

Making it easy also means freeing users from having to remember or look up certain data as much as possible. A good example is the way autocomplete works, when you start typing the name of an ESN user, group, or hashtag. An easy-to-use system will provide a drop-down selection list based on the first characters that you typed. This not only prevents your leaving the current screen to look up any of those values, but it also reduces errors and typos.

Simplicity of the interface can also be useful in other ways, as described earlier. Apart from basic functionality simplicity also supports integration. One discussion we had at SAS focused on the persistence of content, and it was decided to focus the platform on conversation and try to keep the content fairly fresh. In turn, we implemented a policy whereby content was automatically archived after six months. This may seem very short, but any content that is still active (e.g., receiving comments, likes, and so on) will not be archived. In fact, any of those activities will push the archive date back another six months. As a result, content stays fresh and you don't run into many really old posts.

The downside of this policy is that there is an argument that important content will disappear too quickly. The way we are approaching this issue is by encouraging users to take valuable content and make it persistent in the relevant places. For communities this could be a SharePoint team site, for example. We are still fine-tuning that process and have settled on a compromise. There is no perfect solution at this point because we do not want to destroy the conversational elements of the ESN, but we believe that there must be a better way to manage information that must be permanently available.

Simplicity, in this context, means to make it really easy for people to make relevant content persistent. This is a point where automation is usually thrown in as a good approach. Automation is very often seen as a way of getting more done more quickly with the end goal of enhancing overall human performance. The big question with automation is: What is the cut-off point at which humans should take over? Automation can boost performance immensely, but in some cases, if taken too far, it can also lead to a number of issues. For example, it is said that the U.S. financial crisis was partly caused by banks trusting imperfect models instead of relying on due diligence. This reliance on automation caused them to make a number of poor decisions.[1]

Automatic extraction and categorization of content might appear as the ideal solution to the aforementioned issue of making content persistent. The limitation is the quality of the tools performing the task. In a lot of areas, the pattern-matching abilities of the human brain are still better than automatic processes. When we look at automatic translation, for example, it is still not where many would have thought it would be at this point. Finally developers acknowledged that computers do not necessarily translate best when they mimic the human brain. This led to the development of new methods like statistical translation.

Another area where simplicity is a key driver is in making it easy to get content onto a social media platform. One idea that comes up frequently is that of automatic posting. Yes, of course it is easier for an automatic program to pick up some content and post it to a group or other stream in your ESN system. But is that really what you want to do? Do you really want to be responsible for automatically posted comments and posts? Even if the selection model for the posts is very good (often it can run into some glitches, actually), it defeats the social element. Suddenly there is no responsibility or contact for the content (other than the person who designed the feed) and there is no possibility for dialogue. In my experiences, those automatic feeds speak to the more-is-better paradigm again, and while it might be great to have automatic news feeds add to the portal interface of your system, I would be careful with automatically feeding content from other sources into your social media platform. It can reduce the overall quality of the conversation and lead to information overload. It is one thing to get loads of ideas and posts from people, but it is a completely different thing to get spammed by some automatic program hitting you with content. In fact, I decided to un-follow all Twitter users that turned into autofeeds. I specifically want the human element in my social networks.

Automatic posting might make things simpler and easier, but with rising quantity it is likely to reach the point of quality degradation.

MULTIDIMENSIONAL NAVIGATION

As mentioned earlier, technology has given us great improvements in search. Those advancements are not always obvious, as the amount of information has exploded at the same time. So even with improved search algorithms, search tools still have major challenges to return what people are looking for. As a colleague once complained to me, "Who actually needs a *search* engine? What I need is a *find* engine'" The first response to this funny comment might be to point out that you need to search in order to find something. But there are a number of ways to find that do not include search, actually.

One way is to be pointed to content by technology or other users. In the simplest case, this might be a personal recommendation. One common feature of social media tools these days is recommendation. Based on my profile information, my type of activity, my comments, and my type of connections, a recommendation engine can suggest content and connections that might be of potential value to me, personally. The quality of those engines varies but, overall, they are getting better. Automated recommendation started with retail sites. Amazon's list of recommended books based on browsing and buying behavior was just the beginning of what has become a standard feature for many retail sites these days. Even Autotrader.com, a retail automotive company began making recommendations over a decade ago, using browsing behavior as a basis to suggest other kinds of cars shoppers might be interested in.

So it wasn't a big step to try to enhance the experience on social media tools to include automatic recommendation in addition to the user-to-user social recommendations that are so common on those platforms. These social recommendations usually appear in the form of cross-posted content that can be seen by followers. There are two ways this can occur. First, a user can post content on their own page with the intention of recommending it to their followers. Second, a user can post content to another user's page (provided the settings allow it), recommending it to that person specifically and making it visible to both of their followers.

Apart from search and recommendation there are a couple other functions that play a role in finding content and people. Browsing in categories on websites has been a standard strategy for a long time, and it is definitely not dead. In certain taxonomies and catalogs like company directories or group/community directories, search is often paired with the ability to browse a list and select from it. In more recent years, a new type of finding tool—the stream—has evolved from traditional search and browsing. ESNs usually offer a way to channel new content in streams, which are personalized by a user's social media contacts, preferences, and behavior on the platform. Here are some typical streams you will find on social media platforms (no matter if they are external or ESNs):

- **Home stream**. This is where you get all new content that is posted/commented on by all those that you are following.
- **Company stream**. This is usually defined as the complete list of all new posts. In a good-sized company it is very active and posts likely happen in intervals of a few seconds. With the size of the company, streams grow exponentially, so in really large organizations it is usually advisable to use more focused exploration (i.e., custom streams for example).
- **Private streams**. Your posts, your messages, your private replies.
- **Mentions stream**. All posts and comments that include your social media platform user ID. As long as somebody uses the official ID in a post (e.g., in Twitter it is marked with an @ sign, as in @kmjuggler), this stream will pick it up. It can be very interesting as it might show you where you are being quoted or discussed, and this might well be completely outside of your usual channels (e.g., outside of any groups you participate in, outside of your home stream).
- **Custom streams**. Those are more like saved searches that you define based on searching a platform for all content that contains specific keywords or tags. Again, those can be very powerful to find unanticipated content. One will need to manage the keywords properly to avoid getting too many or too little

results back. Also, as tags are not protected or formalized, users can reuse them to mean many different things. This can overwhelm your stream and cause it to display content that has a tag you follow but is completely unrelated to the context you intend. More on tags later in the section.

- **Group/Community streams**. Those are usually focused on all posts or comments that happen in a predefined group or community of practice.

Streams are a great way to organize incoming content. Often the networks have some helpful feature, like indicating that there is news since I last looked at a stream, so I know whether I should look at it now to see new items or not.

Last but not least, I will discuss in more detail what I consider to be the most powerful element of content organization in social media platforms: hashtags. These are also referred to as #tags as the octothorpe (#) is frequently used to identify them. Hashtags are special when it comes to tagging because they are not entered through some type of metastructure (like keywords), but in the content, the text itself. This makes them more convenient to use, even for users who are less technologically savvy.

Twitter users especially are sometimes real artists when it comes to using tags in their short posts. Twitter limits posts to 140 characters, so every letter counts. Instead of posting something like "Knowledge flow management is a great enabler for innovation," you might write "#kfm is a great #enabler for #innovation #km." The resulting post would be picked up by searches looking for any of the four hashtags being used. Some people might not be so familiar with knowledge flow management and still think of it as KM, so adding that extra tag at the end can help ensure the content makes it to the right audiences. Exhibit 7.1 shows how tagging can create connections between content, especially when multiple tags appear in a single post.

What is so amazing about hashtags is the flexibility they provide. Within the content of your platform, every tag creates a new dimension that you can also use to find elements that might be of interest to you (via search or a custom stream, for example). Those dimensions may not be as reliable as a full taxonomy that is managed by experts

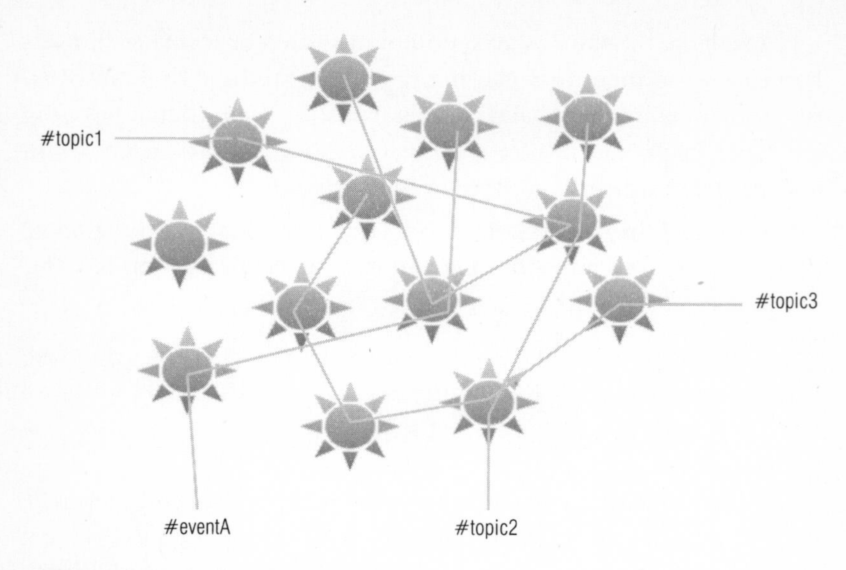

Exhibit 7.1 The Power of Tagging

who ensure consistent content tagging, but they are scaling. The taxonomy approach often has limits when it comes to large, growing, and complex content that changes very frequently. While the downside of hashtags is the lack of full control, the upside is that this allows the space to move very quickly and dynamically to support the change and turnover of the content. Remember that a social media platform is not intended for exhaustive consumption, but rather for discovery. So, it is not a strong requirement that *every* element has to be tagged with the right hashtag to make it useful. You will miss things—that is part of how social media works—and, in fact, it is not so very different to what we experience in the nondigital world, is it? We can and do survive very well without being aware of all possible information around us.

A hashtag may come to life when a certain user uses it for the first time, usually to talk about some content or term that the hashtag is describing for the first time. He essentially becomes a leader at that point. As soon as others pick up the hashtag, it might quickly become a common tag to be used by the larger community, up to the point where certain hashtags are known by almost every user on the platform.

I still remember the first time I saw a Twitter post that used an #FF followed by a number of Twitter user names. #FF is used as an acronym tag (a synonym tag is #FollowFriday) to recommend users (the names listed in the post) that the #FF poster's followers might like to follow as well. It became a common habit to do this on a Friday. #FF became a way of saying, "Hey, it is Friday—why not spend the last hours of the week giving credit to some great Twitter users that provide me with ongoing value by posting great ideas, good links, and more." Since, #FF had already been around a little while when I first came across it, it was easy to find a web page that explained this.[2]

Other hashtags are specifically planned and launched, for example, to be used around certain events. Sometimes an event might use the same tag year after year or make it specific to the year the event is happening. Within organizations, you might see something like #presupdate whenever your organization's president does his quarterly update. Some tags are easy to guess; others you just pick up because you see them in a given context. You might follow a stream or group that is discussing a new topic and see people start using a certain hashtag repeatedly. In the end it becomes common knowledge to use it for this type of topic.

One great way of making common hashtags visible is through trend lists and trend graphs (often in the form of tag lists and clouds). In a list of top trending topics, you find the hashtags that have been used most often in a given timeframe (i.e., the last week or month). Remember from Chapter 1 that a tag cloud is a visualization of top words in a loosely unordered chart, where the most relevant, most used ones are emphasized by bigger fonts or boldfaced words. The bigger and bolded words do stand out and will be easily noticed as leading trends. One feature that both tag lists and tag clouds have in common is that every word is also a link. That link will usually return a search of the content that was tagged with that word.

An example could be a tag like #worklog, which indicated a post where someone basically talks about what they are working on at this moment (other than writing a post on the social media platform, of course). If many people decide to post on their current activities there is a likelihood that #worklog will make it to the top in your tag cloud or tag list. If you would now select #worklog in the list it would actually present you with a list of all those posts that have used the #worklog tag.

This is a great example of how individual activity (adding the tag) results in a new dimension that I can now explore (i.e., what are some of the activities that my colleagues are currently doing?). It is really like the super watercooler that spans your whole organization—a little bit like how you would stand around and ask each colleague, "What are you working on, Bettina in Stockholm? What are you working on, Joe in New York? What are you working on, Nakano in Tokyo?" And by just having a glimpse at each of those activities, a user might get new ideas for their own work, identify potential collaborations, or just get a better view what might be coming down the road.

This type of status information becomes especially important as work is done in smaller chunks (e.g., through agile development in programming work), where leveraging and building on each other's work becomes easier.

The dimensions represented by tags could be within a small area of the ESN or they might span the complete network. What is important to also see is the number of them. There is not really a limit to the number of dimensions being created. Some might dry out if the topic is not as hot anymore or just not catching on, but others might survive for years. Technology plays a great enabler role in exploiting hashtags and your ESN should have a number of features that support the usage, search, categorization, visualization, and measurement of hashtags.

GROUPS OR COMMUNITIES

Social media platforms benefit from structural elements. One of the most important ones is the organization of users into groups or communities. This type of structure is needed, as point-to-point networking will not be enough because it lacks a certain amount of collaboration and direction. Groups help you to get a more visible structure to your network and they are also a great unit of analysis of activity and value.

There is actually a significant difference between a group and a community, especially if we are looking at the more defined structures like communities of practice (CoPs). It is definitely clear that not every group created on a technical platform like an ESN system is a CoP. Unfortunately, it is often used as a synonym by those not fully familiar with what it takes to make a group a full community.

A group in the platform is usually a technical concept describing a number of users who have organized themselves. The group is created by some type of owner or administrator, and users are invited or free to join. Members could learn about it from peers, the group administrator, or a system recommendation.

A group could play a very important role in the overall concept of a CoP, but there are many other important elements that make up a CoP, including clear leadership, sponsorship, and roles (and people that actively fill them), as well as dedicated core community members, events, and activities that give the CoP a pulse.[3] Without these elements, there can still be the technical substructure to support a CoP, but that is not enough to support a true community. In a typical ESN you will have a mixture of those groups that have the backbone of a CoP and those that are, well, just groups. If you really focus on CoPs, you will need a dedicated program to build and manage them. In that case, you could strive to turn most of the groups into real CoPs—but that comes with a cost, so for lighter topics (and especially the work-life social topics) you might never want to go that far. In the startup phase allowing people to create a group very quickly is a pragmatic way to explore the likelihood that a CoP on that topic would be worth the extended effort.

Those community managers that work with ESNs have found that it is necessary to manage groups to a certain degree. In one case, the community manager wanted to create a number of groups before the launch of the platform. This might be a good idea for a few selected topics, but I would be very careful with that approach. An ESN is a great chance for giving something to your organizational members that belongs to them. If they are supposed to invest time and get involved, it is important that they see it as an opportunity for them, personally, to contribute to the organization and the growth of the ESN management. The power of an ESN lies in the self-organization and belief of the users that it really is a forum for them to talk about what they think is important, even though it is not always 100 percent aligned with what management or driving parts of the organization think is important—but therein lies one of the great chances for management to learn from employees deeper down in the hierarchy.

By pre-forming groups, you are again defining the structures for them. I would recommend you give users more of a greenfield and just explain to them what a group actually is, how to create one, and some of the guiding rules around their use. (For more on the importance of guidelines, see the section entitled "Freedom within Borders: The Power of Guidelines" in Chapter 5.) However, what group users think is important should be left to them. Management and other leading departments (like corporate communications) can create groups as examples of what users might find useful, but as soon as you put too much structure into what they are supposed to talk about and what topics they should show an interest in, your efforts are likely to backfire, and might just kill interest in the initiative.

So if there is an urge among your management team to start groups around your most important strategy initiative, push them back at the beginning. If there is enough interest in those initiatives, those who deal with them and have something to say will create groups very quickly. If that does not happen it might be a clear indicator that the strategy is not reaching people, and instead of trying to enforce it via structured conversations, you might need a better overall communication strategy to inform and guide your organization members towards accepting and embracing that strategy.

When getting started in an organizational social network that allows free creation of groups, one tendency I have seen is that people start re-creating what they know. A number of people create groups that are completely aligned with their local organization (e.g.,"Sales Group in Finland" "Consultants in Mexico"). Those groups seem very natural, but they often fall short of some of the benefits. Local groups might have things to discuss, surely, but a lot of that happens at the real watercooler, and to use a group on ESN to just send out news is not the best use of it either. Experience has shown that interest in those types of groups goes down often, because one needs to ask questions like:

- What is the vision?
- What is it that we talk about?
- What energizes us?

Those questions are usually easier to answer when a group is centered on a more concrete topic, like a product, a technology, or a process. And the overall value is usually higher when diverse points of view and experiences come together, which is a lot more likely in a more focused but global topic group than in an unfocused local structural group.

One of the common motivations for launching an ESN in the first place is to bridge certain silos in the organization by introducing horizontal levels of communication that connect the expertise around a given topic from many different parts of the organization. If your group structure just rebuilds those silos in the platform, you haven't won much. Instead of forbidding those types of siloed groups, it is much better to provide a little encouragement for people to create those more driven by vision and interest.

One way to handle this issue is to archive away non-active groups after a given period of inactivity. That could solve the problem in itself. Those structural groups that will stay very active might have a good reason for doing so, and in that case, they definitely deserve to stay up and running and serve their members. However, those groups that show no activity should not be allowed to dilute the overall picture and stay in the system just because there is a real-life structure like that and some people could *potentially* communicate within that group. There should be an ongoing focus to clean up groups that are of no interest to anyone. Getting rid of them usually means archiving or deleting them. This is a task that group owners should take on themselves but, as that often doesn't happen, it is also a task for the community manager to have an eye on groups, suggest consolidation of overlapping groups, or remove those that are clearly not active anymore. Deciding on the consolidation of groups can actually be a nontrivial task sometimes. Setting the scope of a multifaceted topic is like choosing a window to look into a room. Two people might look through different windows into the same room and get completely different pictures, which can convince them that they see two different rooms. The function of the CM could be to show them a top view, where everyone can get a feeling of what the full room looks like. But even then, there is a balance between being very focused on a topic and allowing wide ranges of discussions. Either end of the spectrum has its benefits.

What shouldn't be forgotten in this analogy, however, is that the room is refurbished all the time. So some of the discussion around the scope of groups and whether they should be combined leads from the position of a slow-moving world. The discussion should be led with an eye on the flux of the ESN. Instead of wasting too much time debating if groups should be fused, the focus should be on getting and keeping discussion alive. Most of the time it is better to combine groups and have more traffic that is a little less focused than having specific groups that are hardly active. The argument often given is something like, "There should be more traffic because this topic should interest a lot more people." Well *should* doesn't do it. Either there *is* traffic or there *isn't,* and if there isn't, you should have a close look at how you can increase it. Combining overlapping groups might be one way of doing that.

Many times it is also lack of group leadership (or community leadership) that is the reason why group usage goes down. If a group is just a technical construct without the slightest resemblance to a community that serves people with help and support, defines some purpose, and is managed by some roles, it is more likely that it will decline in usage. Exceptions might be those pure question-and-answer groups, but even those need a frequency of engagement. Without users trusting that someone in a group will answer their questions, they will likely bypass groups and post a question to their followers or the company stream instead, resulting in reduced group traffic.

NOTIFICATION MANAGEMENT

Any social media platform usually wants to become the center of your universe. Facebook would love it if you turned off anything but Facebook and just spent all your time there. They would love you to make it your browser's starting page, the first app in the list on your smartphone, and really the only place you think of going if you want to communicate with your friends and family.

But reality looks a little different. Most users on a social media platform have other channels they use for communication. This is true on an external platform as much as it is internal in organizations.

And if that other tool is email, very seldom (especially in larger organizations and in the early transition phases) will the platform become the universe and only portal for your knowledge workers' activities.

As a result, you will have to deal with a multichannel world. For example, in an organization that is largely driven by email and an Intranet, the Intranet might be completely centralized or divided into divisional and geographic subsites. You might have some chat (maybe via Microsoft Communicator) and the key system that people open up in the morning could be Microsoft Outlook, which they use primarily for email. Now what happens when you launch an ESN as an addition to this landscape? First of all, it is unlikely that people will stop using email—that is, unless you forbid it, which is a rather harsh step. However, this might happen in some smaller organizations with a brave vision to make the ESN the basis for almost everything, but it is not typically the ideal strategy for most organizations.

If Outlook is the center of the universe for people, how do you get them to add the ESN channel to their daily portfolio? One way most organizations do it is via some notification engine that allows them to inform employees in their main platform (email) about what happens in the secondary one (the ESN). So many of the tools come with a range of notification options that allow you to be informed via email if events like the following happen:

- A user follows you.
- A user comments on one of your posts.
- A user comments on one of your comments.
- A user likes one of your posts.
- A new post is added to a group that you belong to or one that you created or own.
- A new group is created.
- The administrator creates an alert to all users.

There is actually a really long list of possibilities, and technically it is really great to have that granularity. Usually you can manage those options via your profile and a good system will also allow you to control the frequency of notification.

While email is a standard option for notifications, at a larger organization with a fast-growing platform, this can overwhelm your inbox, so it is important to manage those notifications properly. Some users will need a guiding hand in doing so.

The types of notifications that make sense to receive depend on a number of factors:

- *Are you a new or seasoned user of social media?* Those who are more experienced might be very good in managing the usage of the network and at methods of getting news from the system in other ways. Casual or inexperienced users might want to enter the ESN world carefully, and getting hundreds of emails that they don't know how to control will likely put a damper on their enthusiasm.
- *Are you new to the platform or new to the organization?* In that case, it might be important to keep the notifications about people following you just to see who is interested in you and the skills you recently brought to the organization. This could be a great way to build a network. If you are a more experienced and long-standing member of your organization, this aspect could be less important.
- *Are there any groups that are central to your current work?* If any of the news and posts within a group could be of high importance to you it surely makes sense to get a notification email on posts and comments.

The way that notifications are being delivered is often configurable between these three basic options:

1. **Immediate**. The second the event happens, you will get an immediate email sent to you.
2. **Daily digest**. Events are collected throughout the day and put into a single email summary that is sent once daily.
3. **Weekly digest**. Similar to the daily digest, but events are collected over the course of a week and summarized in a single weekly email.

Together those notification options provide you with decent flexibility to manage notifications. It is essential that you accommodate those options and, when selecting a platform, you should make it a requirement that users get that flexibility.

There is, however, a downside to making everything configurable: It increases complexity. Many users do not want to dive into a platform that has so many options to manage and think about. By setting sensible option defaults and offering proper training, you can make that process easier for users. Another solution would be to offer workshops or place kiosks in high-traffic areas, where you help people define and manage their profiles and notification settings.

There are actually a few more ways that notifications happen. The most obvious one is streaming. If you go to your home stream (usually the homepage when you enter the platform), you will automatically see new posts at the top. Each of those posts can be seen as a notification in itself, that points directly at a specific message (rather than indirectly as in email). Visual indicators (like little dots or checkmarks) that are placed next to a stream title are helpful in identifying that there is something new in that stream (e.g., posts, comments, likes).

Last but not least, most platforms offer additional pop-up messages that provide information about news in real-time. They do have the tendency of being distracting, but they can be turned on and off during certain times of the day. These pop-up notifications can actually be a good way of getting real-time information about events. For example, if you are involved in a more administrative task and also want to simultaneously follow an event that people are documenting through live posts, comments, and questions, pop-up notifications can be helpful. Instead of following the stream with unbroken focus, you can continue with your administrative task and let yourself be interrupted by a selection of the messages presented (i.e., only those that really interest you).

Notification is a topic that should be taken seriously and it is a good example of how the technology, when used correctly, can be a great enabler—and how, when managed poorly, can represent a big hindrance to productivity. In the end, you want to emphasize the enabler role of technology, exploit the discovery and learning aspects, and minimize distraction.

NOTES

1. David H. Freedman, "Why Economic Models Are Always Wrong," *Scientific American,* posted October 26, 2011, www.scientificamerican.com/article.cfm?id=finance-why-economic-models-are-always-wrong, accessed May 31, 2012.
2. See this blog post on how it all started with a Twitter user called #micah, "Follow Friday. Oh My!" http://learntoduck.com/micah/follow-friday/, accessed May 31, 2012.
3. See my previous book, *Mastering Organizational Knowledge Flow,* for a more detailed discussion on CoPs and the role of a pulse for a KFM initiative.

CHAPTER 8

Social Media Analytics

Measuring programming progress by lines of code is like measuring aircraft building progress by weight.

Bill Gates, Founder and Chairman of Microsoft

ANALYZE WHAT IS GOING ON

If your enterprise social network (ESN) is going to be a success, it will represent one of the major business processes within your organization. Collaboration, knowledge sharing, innovation, person-to-person support, and a considerable part of your organizational culture will be riding on it. Like any other important business process, you should not be flying in the dark about where your ESN is heading and how it performs. You want to measure and track it.

Some effects are easy to measure, and others will seem completely intangible. Douglas W. Hubbard, in his book *How to Measure Anything,*[1] outlines that, with the right approach and clear expectations about precision, it is actually possible to measure things that at first did not seem measureable.

I have used an approach that Hubbard calls Fermi decomposition in my knowledge flow initiatives before.[2] Using this method, you basically get a combination of measured inputs as well as some additional estimates to come up with a fairly good idea of the value of sharing knowledge. One strategy I have used was to build confidence by taking a conservative approach to estimating this value, which was still worth a great deal of money, despite the necessary investment. In fact, the investment costs were actually assessed with a conservative view as well, in that efforts were estimated on the high side.

With a social network there are usually a number of metrics that you get right out of the box as part of the software package. I will go into selecting good key performance indicators (KPIs) in the last section of this chapter, but just to name a few measurements that might be of interest:

- Number of registered users
- Number of connections (follower relationships)
- Number of posts (total, per user, per group, per topic, etc.)
- Percentage of users posting
- Percentage of users commenting on other posts
- Percentage of users reading content
- Hot/trending topics

What all those measures have in common is the fact that they are activity measures focusing on quantitative effects. They do not necessarily say much about the quality of those activities or the potential or real value obtained. As Charlene Li points out in a report[3] by analyst company Altimeter Group, you need to focus on the value. She recommends that organizations:

- Measure gap closing, not engagement.
- Track relationships, not conversations.

The type of measures that will let you focus on value are outcome measures. If you manage to create a reliable link to an outcome based on the flow of knowledge it will be a powerful way of making a business case. One that Bob Buckman mentioned to me is: "Sale of New Products less than 5 years old." Those will work in certain environments but need to be used with care in others. Attributing an outcome to a mixture of influencing activities is not always easy.

Activity measures are straightforward to get. To get those measures that actually represent value, you will have to work a bit harder, and the methods by Hubbard might actually have some answers on how to get there. One way to track relationships is with social network analysis (SNA), and I will go a little deeper into that method later, but this might be a good time to clarify some terminology.

The chapter is called "Social Media Analytics," while the method I just mentioned is social network analysis (SNA). How are those two related, if at all? Social media analytics is concerned with analyzing the activity and effects of connections in social media platforms of any kind. Currently, it is primarily understood as analyzing the activities happening on external social platforms where organizations and individuals interact. Meanwhile, SNA is a specific tool to analyze networks and relationships. You could say that SNA is one tool within the overall framework of social media analytics (SMA). Some other examples of tools related to social media analytics would be the following:[4]

- Social monitoring
- Customer sentiment analysis on feedback
- Predictive analysis used to anticipate certain events

To start out with, I will look at some basic measures typically used to analyze ESN platforms and then see how one might use more sophisticated social media analytics methods.

For a moment let's have a look at activity measures and if they have any value at all. While they might not be good indicators for value (and one of the dangers is, in fact, that people rely on them for indication of value), they can still be useful for assessing what is going on in your network. For one, it is good to track how adoption of the system is in general. How fast is it growing? How well are your marketing initiatives performing in order to get a large portion of your targeted audience to participate? How well are certain divisions, departments, regions, and countries participating? Your targets might differ. Maybe you target only a certain portion of your organization to start with; or maybe you have the expectation that your complete organization will adopt the network as soon as possible. Some of the activity measures can also give an indication that certain groups are adapting much slower than others.

If, for example, you track it by countries (or organizational locations, if you only operate in one country) a comparative report on activity might actually highlight some areas where there is a need for digging in deeper as to why that particular location is using the social network considerably less than others.

Some likely reasons include:

- **Awareness**. For some reason, your rollout of the social network has not reached the target audience in a particular location to the same degree as elsewhere. This might be due to a missing local driver keeping the pulse alive and inform about the platform on an ongoing basis—not only on launch day.
- **Culture**. It might be the general culture that keeps certain people from being open enough to get involved with one of those networks and share their experiences. It could also be a more specific social media culture issue, where people are less familiar with those tools than others and are less social-media savvy. Just like the rate of Facebook users differs from country to country, there are similar differences on internal social media platforms.
- **Local processes**. Depending on how strongly people cling to local processes, they might feel that the social media network is a major shift away from "the way we do things around here." Local processes include competing systems for sharing some of the knowledge that is supposed to be shared on the social media network.
- **Management Support**. The attitudes of senior and middle management towards the social media platform play at least as big a role as awareness and culture. Depending on the strength of the hierarchy of an organization, this might have effects on a local level as well. Are local managers participating in the social media platform, are they ever talking about it? If so, what are they saying? If there is a disconnect between local management and local staff, or if there are local communication issues, it is common for employees to reach out to other parts of the organization to find the communication flow that they are missing.

- **Size of an organization**. Communication is a core process in almost any organization. Location size and the possibilities of interaction with others play a role in how likely it is that someone will get involved with those around them or reach out to the wider organization. (Culture plays into this one as well, of course.) Experts might feel isolated in a small location because they have no one to share their passion with. In that case, the possibility to reach out to like-minded people in other offices becomes a lot easier with a social media platform and it will lead to a higher chance of adoption.

Activity measures might not directly reveal what is behind lower adoption rates, but they are good indicators of where to start digging on a more qualitative level. You could start with interviews and one-on-one conversations with employees at the location. It would be best to travel there and experience the processes, culture, and environment, as that can provide a wealth of information.

Adoption and activity measures need to be taken with care, as mentioned before. Not only do they not necessarily show the actual value, but they can also be deceiving and require further qualification. A typical situation is a gap between adoption and activity. It might well be that there is a high adoption rate (with people signing into the platform and creating a user profile), but that activity drops off very quickly. Reasons could be:

- They don't find the time (or priority) to use the platform on an ongoing basis.
- They are not convinced it does provide value.
- They go back to the old way of collaboration, because that is how they always did it and the new platform seems like extra work.

That is why it is so essential to have an ongoing initiative that will highlight the value of the platform again and again to reach a critical mass of people that are truly *active* on it and who, over time, will encourage their peers (even the skeptical ones) to participate as well.

Activity measures can be useful, but, as mentioned, you need to be very careful with their interpretation and make sure to only see them as a start to the real measuring of value that an ESN might provide to your organization. In order to really understand what is going on, you need to add some value measures.

The reason the majority of organizations do not go beyond the activity measures so far is that it appears to be a bit harder (and potentially more expensive) to collect data for value measures. If you were to constantly ask people to estimate the value of their ESN-based conversations, it could lead to survey fatigue, where people just don't have the time or patience to keep answering questions.

An alternative is to combine certain measures that you already have in a smart way and start interpreting them based on some experiences. One example that Charlene Li names is the idea that a rising number of private groups in a social network indicates a higher degree of maturity, as users go beyond superficial browsing to deeper discussions that might previously have taken place only offline. The privacy of an invite-only group can support this type of communication. This is just one of the signs of a more mature, more entrenched ESN—and it is easily measured.

Another way to obtain value indicators and look at some outcomes is by collecting success stories and assessing the value that each of them brought to the organization. In some cases, this is fairly straightforward. In others it might actually represent a fairly intensive investigation. With The Hub, we used an interesting method to find these success stories. We introduced a special tag named #hubvalue that we recommended people use whenever they reaped a benefit on The Hub (e.g., finding a solution, getting a helpful answer to a question). While the tag does not have a perfect adoption rate, it is used frequently, and with a simple search you find a considerable number of potential candidates for a success story. We could also go ahead and track the number of occurrences of those #hubvalue tags to get a fairly good measurement, assuming that awareness and adoption of the tag is quite high. Otherwise, you might just be tracking the growth of the tag's adoption, but not the growth of successes.

To come back to Hubbard, it would be possible to create a measurement that estimates the average value of a success story (I recommend keeping this conservative) and using it to create a value indicator. This could be measured on an ongoing basis by tracking the number of success stories.

The core questions to ask before jumping into those metrics relate to how these metrics can help your business. So, as Charlene Li puts it, tie your ESN metrics to your highest-value business metrics. If communication is a big issue at your organization and represents one of the issues you plan to fix with an ESN, then you can measure this via a regular internal communications survey. At SAS, one of the key questions we asked was how well users felt informed about company strategy, for example. Differences before and after the introduction of an ESN clearly indicate the effect of the platform—unless there are other parallel initiatives that could confound the results (e.g., growing the number or changing the style of executive webcasts).

Collaboration and interaction are key drivers for success in organizations, and are clearly based on knowledge and innovation. Even in environments that are traditionally not as connected, learning and sharing knowledge becomes more and more important. One approach has been to try to codify the knowledge into documents and share knowledge across the organization in that way. While this codification strategy is still of value in some cases, in the more dynamic organizations it is not always possible (or cost-effective) to try to codify everything for sharing via document or some otherwise packaged asset. The rise of ESNs is an indicator that people are returning to connecting with others to get information to build the knowledge they need.

The output of collaboration comes in many forms:

- A solution that saved a small amount of time.
- Unblocking a hold-up on a project, which can be a small gain or a highly valued project-saver.
- The start of a new innovation.
- An ongoing collaborative effort that leads to a product or a patent, both of which can be valued fairly accurately, but usually with a considerable lag time.

If an organization has this type of collaboration and innovation as one of their key strategies, an ESN would be well suited to support that goal.

Collaboration is also based on trust and relationships. One way to evaluate the effect of ESNs would be to measure relationships. This is usually an activity that is quite expensive and labor-intensive, so the question is: At what level can relationships be measured and quantified? There are some methods, however, that can help assess relationships at a high level, and the most widely used is SNA, discussed in the following section.

SOCIAL NETWORK ANALYSIS VERSUS REPORTING

We are usually tuning our processes to increase efficiency, and a social network is part of this goal. Intruding on social media interactions on an ongoing basis (e.g., sending surveys and follow-up questions to people after they have valuable interactions) might kill the gain in efficiency that you tried to reach by introducing the ESN in the first place. Anecdotes and stories are ways to do some sampling, as I pointed out in the previous section.

But how do you really measure relationships? Usually, you would have to go through detailed interviews to learn about people's relationships, but it is actually possible to learn at least something based on a few selected quantitative measures. Examples might be people's interaction frequency, the number of links they have, the type of subnetworks they are connected to, and so on. Together with additional data on each of the network nodes, there is potential to make real, business-relevant observations.

SAS, the organization that launched The Hub, has been focusing on providing analytics solutions to customers, as well as internally, for many years. In recent years, the company started providing solutions that help organizations to analyze social networks as well.

There are some differences between analyzing a network at an insurance company to detect fraudulent behavior and analyzing an internal social network to get a better feeling of the connectivity of employees. But the techniques to visualize what is happening are very similar in both cases. For an internal social media platform, the goal will be more to view progress (or degress) in the network and to visualize entities. You can visualize follower networks as well as what I would call "posting-links" (i.e., Person A posts and Person B comments, answers, or just refers to Person A). This can be a measured to find the degree of collaboration in the organization. It can show where knowledge could be flowing, albeit not in a direct fashion, as information flow alone does not guarantee knowledge flow and value.

Paired with the analysis of topics and topic clusters, you can actually get a feeling of the communication structures in your organization. But this requires an attitude of trust, and analysis should be always on an aggregated level. It is not only dangerous to go down to the individual level (for legal and trust reasons), but it also would not make much sense, as you want to improve collaboration for the organization as a whole. If there are problem areas, it is a matter of HR and management to go in and investigate those deeper. The task of this type of social network analysis is to provide a high-level overview of what is going on at the moment and where things are predicted to move.

Other types of analytics can analyze topic clusters in order to get an overview and early warning on trends. This can answer questions about whether or not a certain competitor is coming up more often or a particular technology is becoming a trend. You can also use traditional product marketing techniques to get answers to those questions, but the issue is that those holding the knowledge (the crowd out there) might be too busy to answer your questions, and asking them on a daily basis is likely not possible.

Topics being discussed on a daily basis in your ESN can give you that information. Again, it is not about knowing that Joe talked about X and Paula had a question regarding Y; it is more about X or Y being on the minds of a growing group of people and that those topics are trending. This is where knowledge flow management and analytics meet. The output of those types of analytics can make it into dashboards, tag clouds on the Intranet, and be used in the boardroom to include the wisdom of the crowds into the decision-making process.

SNA can also be applied in the more traditional sense, where people are asked questions about their peers. This can happen in either an open fashion, where you start with a certain person or group and follow links that they indicate they have, or in a closed fashion, where you focus on one or more predefined groups and measure the links between them. Those surveys usually focus on only three to five key questions about interactions and relationships, but they still can be fairly labor intensive to score.

When performing SNA-type analytics, the additional data you have available on the nodes in your network (i.e., people) can help you discover answers to questions or just uncover dependencies between certain factors.

Here is an example of how analyzing the data leads can yield some insights and finally provide a sensible measure for your ESN (provided, that you are allowed to evaluate this type of data in consent with your legal and HR departments).

1. You start out by measuring the connectivity of your ESN via follower relationships.
2. As a next step, you merge age and length-of-service information with the relationship data.
3. For privacy reasons, you would then make the nodes anonymous. For the sake of this analysis, it is not relevant who is behind each individual node.
4. Using some graph theory, you could now calculate the average connectivity of members and also analyze it at the level of age group or time with the company.
5. This way you could come to a measurement that would provide insight on connections between old and young colleagues and newcomers and longtime employees.

A bigger mix of age and length of service will help with issues like knowledge lost due to retirement or the successful on-boarding of new employees, both processes seen as important these days.[5] This is only one simple example of how you can create business relevant insights on top of your ESN.

The promise of an ESN is that it might produce interaction indicators from activity data. The activity of following another person is the very first level of connection and relationship, and might reveal some information about connectivity. As always, interpretation has to be done carefully. There is more than one reason why people follow someone else. It could be that they think they must follow a person, not because they are really interested, but because it is their boss or because they feel that they must reciprocate connections with those who follow them.

A relationship of "I am interested in what you have to say" might be only a fraction of all the follow links. A sample survey might help to give you a distribution of those cases, but it also has to be repeated, as the culture might actually change with growing social media maturity.

Here is an example of an error we experienced early on in our social network regarding this measure. There was a feature named Follow All, which was a checkbox that led to a person following *all* new users of the network. There were actually a number of people that checked the flag, underestimating the effect it would have. With the strong growth of the network, some people actually followed more than 7,000 users—clearly not really the idea of following. The company that provided the platform realized the impact of that flag and it was removed from standard profiles. It might have made sense for a very small group of users (say a small organization with 20 people using the platform), but not for a growing population of users at a large organization such as ours. We finally reset the connection lists for those Follow All users and kindly asked them to pick the people they were really interested in from the user registry. This is just one case where a certain feature in the system skewed the results considerably, and why metrics always have to be looked at in quite some detail before relying on them in any way.

A follower relationship is a very light form of relationship. What you might visualize is to what degree those following each other react on other's posts. This can include the number of likes and comments that one would leave on someone else's post in their network. As mentioned in Chapter 5's discussion about network pulse, The Hub recently introduced a feature that allows users to send thank-you notes of different levels and types to others. Those could give additional quality to the follower relationship. But there is a certain element of reciprocity here as well that should be estimated and taken into account.

So far we mainly concentrated on analyzing the network via some type of SNA. But social media analytics goes a lot further. A growing number of organizations are starting to discover the value that this type of analytics provides them with regards to their presence on external social media platforms and there is still a lot of growth potential. As the aforementioned HBR report[6] pointed out, about a third of those engaging in social media activities had not yet measured the effectiveness at all. Knowing what your customers and prospects say about you is so important, however, that the rate of measuring will definitely go up in the coming years.

It is important to understand the difference between simple reporting that looks at the past and sophisticated analytics that can help predict and optimize the future. The latter tools, especially if integrating the data from social media with data from other systems and processes within an organization, can provide a lot more value for guiding an organization in the right direction. Understanding causalities that were discovered through analyzing very large amounts of data can help to react in a way that will open up new opportunities or help avoid crisis situations. The analytical mind is not a nice-to-have option; it is a critical success factor for competitiveness.

Just like how the use of social media has moved from external environments into organizational environments, analytics should follow along. ESNs of tens of thousands of employees are becoming more and more common, as it is those large organizations that are most likely to create silos that need connecting. Even if there are only a few hundred users on your ESN, it is worth it to start looking at the data with an analytical eye, but with networks of thousands, data quickly gets really big. With the right analytical mind-set and tools, there are a number of opportunities, not only to fine-tune your ESN for effective usage, but also to use it as a detection engine for trends in a more general business sense.

James Surowieki talked about the use of prediction markets in organizations in his book, *The Wisdom of Crowds*.[7] One of the downsides of prediction markets is that they need active participation, which requires yet another effort (prediction markets are similar to betting games, which might actually be fun to do, but not everyone will see it that way).

In contrast, analytics of social media content can work with what is already there. There are important differences in some of the measures you should be looking at and especially how you look at them, as I pointed out in the section on motivations in Chapter 2. Social media analytics is still developing on the external side, and taking the next step to apply it to your ESN would give you a head start over other organizations that are not at that level yet. I predict that social media analytics in larger ESNs will become as common as those networks themselves, and organizations will become more mature in running them in the future.

CHOOSING THE RIGHT KPIs

Measuring the value of knowledge flows is not easy, and one should be rather careful in approaching it. In the previous section, I introduced some example measurements and tools that will help you get some insight into your ESN and where it is heading. However, one of the key questions is what some of the most useful measurements—also called KPIs—might be. In her Altimeter report, Charlene Li pointed to the fact that one should concentrate on metrics that symbolize some closing gaps between issues in the organization rather than participation metrics.[8]

The most frequently used way to assess the closing of business-issue gaps is via surveys. One of the downsides of surveys is that they can lead to survey-fatigue, where people just get fed up with filling them in all the time. So, while I fully agree that those measures are the most valuable ones to have, there is a limit as to how many of them you can have without annoying your users to the point where only a fraction of people will answer, skewing the results.

In the end, you will have to use a balanced set of metrics. Participation measures alone will be insufficient. They might be able to tell you something about the number of people in the organization who are aware of the system, but how many of them are engaging in valuable conversations is a different kind of question. Measuring the ratio between those that are actively contributing to the ESN and those that are merely reading other content is a more useful metric.

As with any of the other measures, you need to be very careful when you look at targets for them. In this example, one might assume that it would be good to strive towards 100 percent participation. In a couple of example ESNs that are considered to be running quite well, I have seen that roughly about 10 percent of users were active contributors, and 70 to 80 percent were readers, even after a year. This can actually be okay. It depends in part on your adoption rate in comparison to the complete organization. You could have an adoption rate of 1 percent, and even if 100 percent of those are actively contributing, it wouldn't tell you much about the overall connectivity of the organization because the community is too small. The ratio of contributors to consumers will very likely be below 100 percent if you have a larger and diverse audience. It lies in the human nature that some people are more likely to participate through contribution than others. The targets for measures like that should be looked at very closely and you will also need to adjust those targets as things progress.

One example measurement that Charlene Li mentioned in the report is to what degree employees might feel connected to executives, and if an ESN can reduce that power gap.[9] Similarly, you could take the distance values between old/young and new/longtime employees.

There are some types of measures that are a lot more general and fall into the outcome measure category. For example:

- Number of patents
- Number of new products developed based on collaborative efforts between one or more people from separate locations
- Shareholder value

The issue with those measures, even though they represent real value, is that it is often quite hard to attribute the proper amounts to a single initiative, like the ESN in our case. This would really only work if the ESN were the only parameter that changed, which is unlikely in today's dynamic organizations. In the case of patents, for example, there could be a range of reasons why there is suddenly an increase of them. Better communication and collaboration might be one of those reasons, but how reliable is it to put a value on the exact contribution of a single factor?

Another category of measures can be derived from specific content. You will remember how at SAS we introduced a special #hubvalue tag for users to indicate in the stream of messages that they received real value from a post or comment. So you could actually count the number of #hubvalue tags and see whether they are increasing, for example. Again, the conditions under which people actually use that tag might be significant. Did they know about the tag? How many people actually use it? How many do not use it, even though they derived value from a post? A number of unknowns might make the result hard to interpret.

One measure I consider rather useful is the average speed to an answer. If someone asks a question, how long does it take until a reply or answer is posted? The average speed of reaction could be compared to other systems like an internal problem-tracking system. What it does not include, though, is an evaluation of the real value of that answer. For example, if you were to make that measurement visible to all participants and request that questions get quick responses, the effect could well be that a certain fraction of users would shoot back a quick reply that they did not properly research, just to fulfill the speed requirement. The result would be worse service even though the speed measurement would appear to show an improvement.

An indication of the value of a post or answer can be communicated with a like button. That is the shortest form of feedback that needs the least effort to use, which is probably why likes are more common than comments. Especially with the rise of mobile devices, where it is somewhat awkward to type a long comment, it is simple to hit a like button. Evaluating the frequency of hits can be a good indicator for activity as well as how many people liked certain answers, and value can also be evaluated by investigating which topics and hashtags produce predictions about certain trends. To interpret the quality of this data, you will need to be careful to not misinterpret writing ability for content. Some of the posts might be irrelevant or off-topic, but they could get a lot of attention (e.g., likes, comments) because they happen to be funny or well written. Most often it is a good strategy to look for a combination of content (e.g., an interesting, relevant topic) and tone (e.g., nicely said). As long as you are aware of those two dimensions, analyzing like buttons could really add to the understanding.

One interesting measurement that Charlene Li mentions in her study is the ratio of private (closed) groups in comparison to public groups. She argues that a rise in the number of private groups is an indication of the maturity of an ESN.[10] When I first read that, my reaction was skeptical, as I would have thought that the creation of private groups would have been something that people were more likely to do when they are new to an ESN and don't want their discussions fully exposed. Especially when groups are created in complete alignment with existing organizational structures, I would still see that as a motivation to make groups private. However, when an ESN gets beyond the first bootstrap phases, I do see her point. The maturity of an ESN is also based on the degree to which those offline conversations migrate to the online world. The more this happens, the more likely it is that people will also need private rooms to discuss things that are confidential or not ready for wider distribution. Privacy is also preferred by a group that puts a large emphasis on focus and, therefore, wants to determine and limit the audience.

What I always find important is to have a portfolio of KPIs that balance each other to provide a more complete picture. Activity could give you one little piece of the story, and evaluation and comments can supply another piece. Also, when you are not 100 percent sure how to interpret certain measurements, a fallback strategy could be to look more at trends than at absolutes. Often it is more revealing to discover growth rates rather than usage rates. Similarly, to follow numbers over time it can be quite interesting to look at them in geographic perspective (and, similarly, by organizational entity). Comparing numbers from country to country could reveal information that will help you learn more about how and why your users are using the ESN or not. What could be the reason that the French office is contributing three times as much as the German office? By feeding back some of the results, you can also create some type of competition. You can also plan events around the data, like a company-wide brainstorm, where people generate as many ideas as possible in a given timeframe. This could be measured in a competitive way to designate a winning office or team. Keep in mind that these types of events encourage quantity and not necessarily quality, but such rare single events might raise the ESN's visibility and adoption rate (two metrics you will want to track).

One way to measure overall connectivity within an ESN is to look at brokers and how they develop. Brokers are users who are very active, have large networks, and make it a habit to lead people to other users. The number and activity level of brokers can be an indicator of how connected the overall network becomes. If you are aware of certain silos you could measure this specifically by looking at individual brokers within each of your organizational silos. And as an action item have the CM (community manager) encourage broker functions within parts of the organization known for showing silo behavior.

As some of those examples have shown, choosing the right KPIs is not always easy. It is most important that you check the hypothesis behind a measure regularly to make sure that a measure indicates what you expect it to. This can be done through small surveys or just by talking to users and other stakeholders on a regular basis.

NOTES

1. Douglas W. Hubbard, *How to Measure Anything: Finding the Value of Intangibles in Business, 2nd Edition* (Hoboken, NJ: John Wiley & Sons, 2010).
2. Frank Leistner, *Mastering Organizational Knowledge Flow: How to Make Knowledge Sharing Work* (Hoboken, NJ: John Wiley & Sons, 2010), Chapter 8, "Measure and Analyze."
3. Charlene Li with Alan Webber and Jon Cifuentes, "Making the Business Case for Enterprise Social Networks," Altimeter Report, posted February 22, 2012, www.slideshare.net/Altimeter/altimeter-report-making-the-business-case-for-enterprise-social-networks, accessed May 31, 2012.
4. See "The New Conversation: Taking Social Media from Talk to Action," A report by Harvard Business Review Analytic Services, 2010.
5. For information on the value of fighting loss of knowledge, see David DeLong, *Lost Knowledge: Confronting the Threat of the Aging Workforce* (New York: Oxford University Press, 2004). For information on the value of onboarding, see Mark Stein and Lilith Christiansen, *Successful Onboarding: Strategies to Unlock Hidden Value Within Your Organization* (New York: McGraw-Hill, 2010).
6. See "The New Conversation: Taking Social Media from Talk to Action," A report by Harvard Business Review Analytic Services, 2010.
7. James Surowieki, *The Wisdom of Crowds: Why the Many Are Smarter Than the Few and How Collective Wisdom Shapes Business, Economies, Societies and Nations* (New York: Doubleday, 2004).
8. Charlene Li with Alan Webber and Jon Cifuentes, "Making the Business Case for Enterprise Social Networks," Altimeter Report, posted February 22, 2012, www.slideshare.net/Altimeter/altimeter-report-making-the-business-case-for-enterprise-social-networks, accessed May 31, 2012.
9. Ibid.
10. Ibid.

CHAPTER **9**

What's Next

The best way to predict the future is to invent it.

Alan Kay, Computer Scientist

ADVANCES IN TECHNOLOGY

Making an ESN successful takes a lot more than technology, but as I mentioned before, technology and processes associated with technology can and will have a considerable impact. Some technologies will be game changers by making certain things easier and adding new capabilities.

Technologies that typically make a difference impact the human–computer interface, bridging the gap between eye movement, gestures, speech, and voice. The barrier of language will slowly but eventually break down through the use of better translation algorithms, like statistical translation.

Eventually there will also be a bridge between a device and a user's real-world environment through holograms, keyboards that are beamed onto a surface, and gestures that control things. You will not even have to touch a computer, anymore. These technologies already exist, though they are in limited use (often by the physically handicapped), and will someday become mainstream. And this day might be closer than we think. At the time of writing this book a new motion tracking device was just announced by a company called Leap Motion to be available around the end of 2012. It cost less than $100 and Leap Motion claims it can track hand movements down to a 1/100th of a millimeter. Technologies like these have the potential to considerably change the way we interact with computers.

There are even ways to move and manipulate computer-generated content with your mind. Some of this will be scary, but when trains first came along people were seriously concerned that we would suffer immediate brain damage from traveling at the speed of 50 miles per hour.

From a social media point of view I am hoping for developments that will make connecting with each other even easier through a better integration of content and conversation. This calls for certain types of automation, and a lot will be about using metadata. The big question will be how to categorize content and give it meaning.

The semantic web will finally become a reality on a wider scale because people will have simpler ways to communicate. Innovative ideas will make the management of folksonomies more realistic. New ways to present content—variations and extensions of what we know as tag clouds—will make it a lot easier to navigate the many dimensions that tags create across the network.

In the end, it will still be important to find the one person who has the knowledge that you need, but instead of doing clumsy searches, there will be multiple ways of drilling for information. Today, having multiple ways into content and human networks is still a luxury and the number of interfaces can be overwhelming. In the future those will be very easy to customize on the fly. They will be customizable by anyone, not just technical experts, and even better interfaces will self-train and customize themselves in an intuitive way.

The basic idea is not new. One typical application of it started years ago with recommendations at Amazon; people who bought this book also liked that one. Social networks followed with recommendations for people to connect with and posts to read. As analytics become so much more integrated into everything we do, it will also help with searches, browsing for content, and connecting to individuals.

But for these technologies to succeed, they have to be very much aligned with what we know on a small scale. Artificial environments that change on the fly are not necessarily desirable. I still think with horror of the feature on Microsoft Word that rearranges the order of tabs based on what was last used. There were 10 or 15 tabs and every time you hit one, they all rearranged. Some smart developer had the idea it would be good to have the one that was last used on the bottom left, but the changing tab order was a nightmare, as you would have to search all of them again and again to find any tab other than the one you last used. This shows that there are different ways of looking at a problem, and the most practical one might not be the most user-friendly. In the end what counts is people and how they work.

Another recent movement that is indicative of what we will be seeing is statistical translation. For quite some time, automatic translation has been predicted to be around the corner. But even Moore's law with the exponential growth of computing power has not yet provided usable machine translation. Most of it is still pretty bad. But now that we have rather large computing power, new things are possible by taking a completely new approach. Instead of trying to figure out sentence structures, statistical translation takes whole fragments of sentences and translates them based on historical translation, using statistics to decide which might be the best way to translate a sentence. It is a little bit like chess programs that analyze every possible move instead of trying to behave like the human mind. Yes, algorithms are still important and can be used, but immense computing power also makes it possible to follow more than one route at the same time because machines can.

Another example of where things are heading is a recently launched digital camera from Nikon, the Nikon 1. The magic behind the camera is that it anticipates future actions by the photographer. The original developments in digital photography offer some other great examples. I still remember how it changed photography for me personally. At 70 cents a picture I would often think twice before shooting a photo. Spontaneity was a luxury that only professional photographers could afford. For them, running through 20 rolls of film was just part of their business and the cost would be more than offset by the services they got paid for. For the amateur, this was usually not an option. At one point I remember that picture developing services would let you to go through your developed pictures, give back those that didn't turn out, and pay for only the ones you kept. For this type of service you would usually pay a premium per picture, but the idea was going in the right direction, and it was used as a competitive sales tool.

The quantum leap of choice came with digital cameras. With digital photography suddenly you could take 5, 10, or 20 pictures of the same thing and delete the ones you didn't like. The only costs are associated with battery life or hard-drive space, and these have gotten cheaper as technology has advanced. Today's costs per picture are in a completely different range than the 70 cents I paid in the past.

But cost is only one aspect in this development. Another aspect is speed. The Nikon 1 was the first to offer a new feature called Smart Photo Selector Mode.[1] If you just slightly press the shutter it starts taking up to 20 high-speed pictures. Once you actually press it, it saves the best four shots based on some algorithms (e.g., eyes open, no red eyes, no glare) and then presents those for you to choose your personal favorite. What a great example of technology anticipating, providing options, and letting the human make the final decision.

This could be a great model for other uses of technology. Another example in a similar direction is the way that Google and other search applications present a variety of search results based on what you type into the search field. With growing computing power, you can use smart analytical methods within seconds and on a sublevel, where increasing the speed of returning results is important. You might not care as much about the fact that a search comes back in 0.350 seconds versus 0.410 seconds, but you do care when the results are considerably more targeted, better fitting what you wanted to know.

Just recently Google announced the first product out of its Project Glass line,[2] a pair of glasses (or an add-on for your standard pair) that will make it possible to see web information blended in to the world as you look at it. You can also take pictures and videos directly from the tiny camera in the glasses. One use of such a technology is augmented reality (AR), which presents information based on the surroundings I am looking at. This could be driven by GPS information or image recognition of the entity I am looking at (e.g., a house, a person, an object).

In the first television demo[3] Sebastian Thrun, the development lead on the project and head of the Google(x) research lab, explained that Google does not currently see augmented reality as the main driver for it, so much as the community aspect of sharing what one sees, immediately. There is no need to take a picture and upload it to Facebook, Google+, or any other social media platform. You start your video or take a picture just by pushing a button on the glasses. You get a choice of people to share with and nod to share it. Maybe a future version will be operated by thinking of certain people and confirming what you'd like to send them. An internal social media platform could one day offer similar functionality.

What is intriguing about the concept of the glasses (let's leave the brain steering to the future for a minute) is the fact that it centers around individuals and what they experience in real time. It is not connected to a certain application. Let's take the example of sharing links, pictures, or videos. Currently, I still have to make the link from one system to another using a button or special feature on the application that I am using. For example, my current web browser has a button to share things on The Hub in one click. If I use a different web browser, will it have that button, too? Or is the feature platform-dependent, meaning a sharing functionality has to be available on several different platforms that I am using over the day, including my smartphone, my tablet, or my multimedia TV system.

An application I can envision would be reading a book (e-book or paper) and when I find an interesting quote, I just point my glasses at it, highlight the quote with my fingers, and say "Share" to post it to my social network. Imagine if, by looking at the title, a link would be added to the post so users would be able to reference where the quote came from. Similarly, I could look at content on a web browser and copy the URL to easily share the link.

The video element of those glasses also holds a lot of power. We spend less and less time building knowledge based on written documents, which is why there is a big trend of sharing via video. Short, precise videos with messages not longer than 5 to 10 minutes are mainstream for learning and sharing these days. There are already a considerable number of those type of educational videos on YouTube, where you can learn about anything from juggling to baking a cake, and, in fact, this is how children learn these days. They just look up a video on YouTube and go for it.

Another great example of this trend is the phenomenal success of the Khan Academy, a nonprofit online academy founded by Salman Khan in 2008, which is currently offering over 3,000 educational videos that have been watched a combined 150 million times. This same trend is moving into organizations. At SAS, the use of videos is definitely trending—for informational as well as educational purposes—and currently the internal web team is looking at redesigning the Intranet to feature videos more prominently.

If we combine that idea with the video glasses mentioned, it would make it really easy to record an instructional video with sound while you do something. No camera to set up. You could even live stream what you are doing with your audio comment. There are no delays in sharing that knowledge.

Imagine an oil company where one of the most experienced oil-rig experts moves out to a platform to fix a problem. Depending on the weather, this can be an effort that could be unpleasant or even dangerous. By pushing a button the expert could live-stream what he is doing to the ESN for the benefit of others, who would experience what he is experiencing (vision, sound, vibrations, and more) live, while he is going through the exercise of trying to find and fix the problem. Even if he runs into a dead end, people will walk with him and learn from it, as he learns from his experience.

I am not sure if we will all run around with those types of glasses in a few years, maybe there is a whole different way of doing this in the future, but the direction of making sharing technology seems a likely one at this point.

DEALING WITH CHANNEL OVERLOAD

One trend that I have seen in the last few years is that people increasingly suffer from what I would call channel overload. Tools and platforms are being launched at an increasing speed, and as different people communicate on different channels, there is a certain pressure to follow several of them at the same time. With external social media tools, a good example would be people following LinkedIn, Xing, Facebook, and Google+, all at the same time, as not everyone they want to interact with is on the same platform. Different people will have a different focus and if you really want to keep up, you will have to go multichannel. The same is true within organizations. As users move through channels at increasing speed, one channel that was mainstream only a year ago is suddenly replaced by another.

The question is when to jump over to this other thing. As a result, people jump at different times, and multiple channels co-exist.

Another reason they will co-exist is functionality. One channel will be slightly more suitable to use for certain types of communication than another one. Even if they start out with a similar focus, there is always that one feature that is better or worse and, depending on how important it is to you, you will stay or leave earlier or later.

I don't anticipate channel overload to become any better in the near future, but rather think it will get worse. The solution from an application provider is easy of course: Just use my tool and forget about all the other ones. While this message might be appealing, the fights for the one-and-only tool will be fierce and, with new innovations coming along at increasing speed, each of them having something to add, and development speeds that are different from vendor to vendor, I am quite sure a growing number of channels will still be an issue for a while, and channel overload a pain we will suffer.

One approach to reduce it would be extended training. Helping people on a daily level to position and define the channels and understand what each is good at. Then, we can help individuals build a channel portfolio that fits their needs and keeps overload at a minimal level.

A different method to deal with channel overload is to make certain channels beat out others by intensifying marketing activities and showing the attractiveness of those channels. The strategy could be to move some traditionalists off the older channels to a selected set of newer ones. As a result, networking could happen based on a smaller set. You could of course force certain channels as well, but I would not recommend it as people will find ways to circumvent the decision if they don't really believe in it.

Managing the channels does not only mean reduction, but also using the ones that are there in an effective manner. To a certain degree, people can be trained on that. The other input to a successful model is discipline, something that people will have to a varying degree. The way that people use certain channels in combination with others can also spread through the organization like anything else in an ESN via the examples, stories, questions and answers, special events, and much more. Good practices can develop and should be shared and groups and communities of users can develop those practices collaboratively.

MORE SOCIAL OR MORE TECHNOLOGY

A lot of the success of social media is based on the connection of what we are good at. Since the early times of man, we have been social and using tools that scale social interaction to wider audiences than ever before. It is the point, when people really realize this power, that they become intrigued and start looking for ways to leverage it.

One question for the future will be: How will those two areas develop in relation to each other? Will technology take over more and push the social bits aside? Or, will we see a renaissance of social interaction driven by smarter technology that does actually try to get out of the way as much as it can and do its job more silently in the background?

There is a balance that needs to be hit. In *Mastering Organizational Knowledge Flow,* I called it the human–technology continuum. If you look at the recent success of Apple versus Microsoft, for example, it can be explained by setting more focus on the social side and less on technological features. Part of the success of iPhones and iPads (apart from great marketing campaigns, of course) was the fact that those devices introduced new levels of simplicity. They passed a threshold of ease regarding use of mobile devices and were able to get enough people to experience their devices hands-on in stores. I once watched an older gentleman have his first run with an iPad and, walking slowly out of the store, he murmured with disbelief that, "This is really magic." I have had parents tell me how their four-year-olds use multiple learning apps completely by themselves with no instruction. When the father of a friend of mine got one of those devices at age 80, a new world of reading newspapers, watching his grandchildren's pictures, and even sharing funny YouTube videos opened in a phase of life when you might not necessarily expect it.

The more complex our lives get from the point of view of interaction, the more simplicity we need in the tools and platforms we use.

In recent years, a growing number of knowledge experts have realized that the growth of complexity within organizations calls for new approaches. One definitive leader in that area is Dave Snowden, KM pioneer and founder of the CognitiveEdge Network. He developed the Cynefin framework,[4] which approaches organizational complexity with a range of innovative methods, many of which are based on the power of narrative and story. One of his key messages is that the old paradigm of fail-safe environments is an illusion and does not deal properly with complexity. A fail-safe environment would be one where no errors may happen. Instead, he proposes to create safe-to-fail environments, within which errors and mistakes are allowed and part of the system.

There are multiple areas where this paradigm comes to play. When you think of organizational leaders not allowing their employees to participate in external social media or any internal open communication platform, it is very often that they are afraid of things going wrong. They want to control the environment to a point where no errors can happen. As I pointed out earlier, even with those kinds of strict rules, information will slip out in other ways, so it is clearly a naive view to think one could control the system to a fail-safe state. It is a better approach to set a more open framework (via guidelines that are simple enough for people to understand and follow) and have them move relatively freely within that framework. Any incidents are part of risk management, and you need to deal with them when they happen. Especially since very often the risks are not assessed accurately (those accessing them often underestimate peer-control, for example), this approach delivers considerably more value over time. A fail-safe attempt will stifle a lot of innovative powers.

One important social aspect of social media is that of privacy. The range of opinions on this aspect is rather wide. On one end of the spectrum, you have people announcing that privacy is an old concept and that we are all public individuals these days. On the other end of the spectrum, there are those that really want to push back on collection and distribution of personal information. The discussion itself could fill several books and I, personally, think this is another one of those areas that we need to manage and constantly try to find a good balance for.

Some of the factors that usually influence people's position on privacy are:

- **Age**. Our children grow up with tools like Facebook and exposing their private lives is something they get used to, though this is plainly underestimating dangers.

- **Culture**. People in some countries (like Germany or in some Asian countries) are often more sensitive than in the United States, based on their political views and how skeptical they are in general.
- **Background**. Fear usually comes from the unknown.
- **Prior (bad) experiences**. Those who have been hit by identity theft of any kind are a lot more likely to be careful in the future.
- **The number of (published) incidents that result in damage**. Publicly reported cases of privacy invasion (stolen credit card numbers, identity theft) do influence some people to take at least a closer look.

As with many other powerful tools the power cannot only be used for the well-being of others but also for criminal intent. Usually within organizations, there is less of a chance that this is the case, mostly as it is usually a lot easier to find the originator that might be misbehaving. Specifically on ESNs, users are named and otherwise identifiable. Nevertheless even in those environments privacy plays a role. What about confidential data about performance salary or position? What about pictures and how they get shared? Those are areas that need to be looked at and be dealt with. Social does not mean that anything that has to do with social interaction is also politically and legally correct. That is one of the reasons why it is and remains so important that those running an organization's social media efforts stay in close contact with some legal guidance.

I want to close this section with a quick discussion on whether technology changes organizational culture. Personally, I believe that technology does actually have the potential to change how we socially interact. It only takes a quick look at today's teenagers to see how texting and Facebook has changed some of the ways that they communicate with each other. To a certain degree the same is true in organizational settings. However, this should not serve as an excuse that technology be introduced without any guidance and strategy. The saying "if you build it, they will come" is based on the misconception that the sheer existence of a technology will mean it will get adapted and used in a productive manner. It needs both the technology but also those people that help manage the knowledge flow and look at the human and social side of their usage.

INTERACTION TRENDS

In recent years it has become harder to say exactly what is inside an organization and what is outside. Companies have outsourced not only standard processes but also processes like innovation, sometimes having the crowd help them develop a service or product. Also, the complexity of interaction means that teams between one organization and its partners become rather close. Where there was a fairly clear boundary between companies only a couple of decades ago, some cross-organizational teams are more closely related than similar teams internal to the same organization. It could also be that a cross-organizational team is competing with an internal team in a different division of that same team. This not only goes for partners—in some cases, the lines are blurry between an organization and its customers as well. The defining element is not structure but topic (e.g., work product, project, know-how) and interactions move from competition to *coopetition* (see Exhibit 9.1).

As these cross-organizational collaborations need communication, it is clear that this will have an effect on the scope of ESNs. Actually, that term might be not completely correct at that point, unless you see those partners as an extension of an enterprise's ecosystem. Then again, it is usually still the enterprise that runs it and decides on the type of partners or customers it will allow into it and which ones it will keep outside.

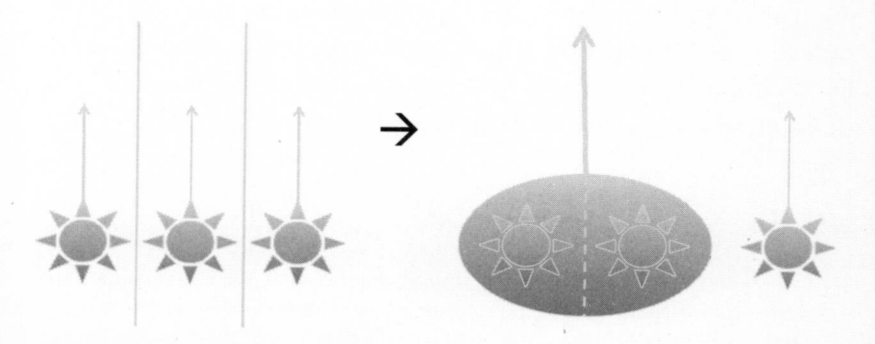

Exhibit 9.1 From Competition to Coopetition

One interaction trend that is definitely visible is a further extension of mobile. Smartphones are everywhere these days, tablets are definitely on the rise. A phone is nice and small and easier to carry with you, but with their extended screen space and limited space and weight, tablets just open up a lot more possibilities. Typing with a larger keyboard, applications that can not only show one stream but several increase the usability to a point where managing your ESN or social media presence from anywhere, anytime, is now possible.

Sounds like we are almost there. The limiting factors at the moment are still holes in the wireless network. As long as you can pay 100 times[5] more for roaming in another country than in your own, there is still a barrier that I hope will fall with more airports and hotels going to free wireless. Still, I think there will be a move to the always-on society. Just like how, at least in high-technology countries, no one discusses whether there is power in your house or not, it is expected to be there.

Interaction is characterized by collaboration and a 2010 study by the Future Foundation[6] found there is an 81 percent positive correlation between collaboration and innovation. Therefore, enhanced collaboration is also an indirect driver for competitiveness. The article mentioning the study also concluded that it will need for IT and HR to come together in the role of a Human Systems Director. So far it has been a responsibility of a CKO (chief knowledge officer) to build that bridge between HR and IT, but that only works as much as either one of those two divisions opens up towards the other one, and both functions are often still solely focused on their daily business with no time to devote to look at something exotic as systems (from an HR point of view) and people issues (from an IT point of view). Creating a function with the specific responsibility at the executive level seems like a radical step for many organizations, but it would be just the kind of devotion collaboration will need.

NOTES

1. See Nikon's website for more information: www.nikonusa.com/Learn-And-Explore/Nikon-Camera-Technology/gst5xlzp/1/Smart-Photo-Selector-Mode.html, accessed May 31, 2012.

2. By the time this book is published, I am sure there will be people running around with them.
3. Sebastian Thrun interview on Google's Project Glass, posted April 27, 2012, www.youtube.com/watch?feature=player_embedded&v=FzpCcJ8sXik#!, accessed May 31, 2012.
4. See http://cognitive-edge.com, accessed May 31, 2012.
5. In Switzerland I currently pay about 50 Swiss francs (1CHF=$1.10) for 1GB of data usage. If I travel to Germany, the same 1GB would cost me 5000 Swiss francs via roaming. And certain hotels in Germany charge you more than $20/day for wireless.
6. Siân Harrington, "Google Research Heralds Arrival of the Human Systems Director," posted June 10, 2010, www.hrmagazine.co.uk/hro/news/1017971/exclusive-google-research-heralds-arrival-human-systems-director, accessed May 31, 2012. See also the original study, Bob Little, "The Human Systems Director: New Skills Help Foster Collaborative Corporate Environments," posted August 2010, http://elearnmag.acm.org/archive.cfm?aid=1852160, accessed May 31, 2012.

CHAPTER 10
Final Thoughts

Sharing knowledge is not about giving people something, or getting something from them. That is only valid for information sharing. Sharing knowledge occurs when people are genuinely interested in helping one another develop new capacities for action; it is about creating learning processes.

Peter Senge, MIT-based author, researcher, and educator

Whether you skipped to this last chapter or you made it through the whole book, I want to leave you with a few final thoughts.

In the previous chapter, I outlined some potential developments in the future and pointed out that some of those might be just guesses. It is very hard to predict certain developments in this field, and it is even harder to say what will come next, as some developments take a lot longer to be successful and others occur more quickly than anticipated. For example, tablet PCs were around for over 20 years, but they had little success until simplicity and touch technology finally led to the iPad and an incredibly fast adoption rate, with millions of tablets making it into consumers' and business users' hands.

When adoption is slow it is easy to fall into the trap of putting down a development as a failure, but maybe it is just not ripe or certain features are missing that are delaying a mainstream success. This can happen if a feature depends on technology that is not yet developed or connected. Other times it is that users are just not ready to make that jump into something that seems radically new.

What does this mean for your initiative? The key is to stay flexible, employ additional tools, and watch the reactions of your users. By locking yourself into platforms that are too large and inflexible to change, you can lose the competitive edge that those tools can provide. You cannot simply launch and be done for the next 20 years; you must take in new streams of ideas and experiment in pockets, whether those new tools and the processes that come with them are of potential benefit to your organization.

This means you have to hit the right balance. Having a clear strategy outlined as a framework is still very important, and so are grassroots developments that come from your organization's frontlines. After allowing these grassroots developments, you must still make a conscious decision whether you want to launch another social media tool to the full audience, however. Otherwise the danger is that your users end up with ever-increasing channels, overload, and confusion.

But in all of this it is important to be always clear and remind oneself every day of the key phrase: "Technology alone is not the answer!"

It is very easy to get hung up with the platform itself, and forget about the most important factor in all of this, which are the users. They are what will make it work (or not) in the end. An environment that is characterized by trust, open communication, and a proper work-life balance is the key driver for people sharing their knowledge. Once that mind-set is there, the tool will make a difference as to the speed at which adoption happens. If you just push the technology into an organization that is missing most of those environmental conditions, it is likely to fail. But even in those organizations that do not yet have the proper environment it could be of value to at least experiment with certain social media tools. You could use them to show successes that could change the way some executives view these tools and the opportunities they present.

An executive-level change of mind can lead to opening up even wider because an organizational culture is driven largely from the top. Small steps to change the culture could be a great step in the right direction.

The reward of going through this journey and reaching the stage of a well-run and widely used enterprise social network (ESN) can be manifold:

- Better and faster answers for questions drawn from the full diversity of your organization.
- Agility and speed in performing business processes.
- Increased collaboration linked to increased innovation.
- A better sense of global connectivity for members of your organization (and also key partners or customers, if you decide to open it up to them).
- Increased attractiveness for the next generation of talent, a generation that expects this type of connectivity, not only in their private lives but also increasingly in business.

The overall result will be an organization that is better suited to face the growing challenges of market dynamics and competition.

Every day new experiences around ESNs and social media are being made within and across organizations. It is a topic that is increasingly researched by universities, as well; therefore a book can provide only a snapshot. As I would like to learn from you, I hope you will engage with me on my blog (http://masterknowledgeflow.blogspot.com/), where I plan to highlight some of the experiences that I will surely have over the coming years. I invite you to share some of your experiences and comment on the posts, and see where our collaboration takes us.

Appendix A
Key Success Factors

Simplicity is the ultimate sophistication.

Leonardo DaVinci (1452–1519), Italian Renaissance architect, musician, inventor, engineer, sculptor, and painter

After reading this book, you should have a good idea of what some of the key factors are to keep in mind when you want to introduce an enterprise social network (ESN) and make it successful over time. For convenience and as a reference, here is a summary of those factors that have shown to be of relevance.

Leonardo DaVinci stated one of the most important success factors that you should keep in mind 500 years ago. He had great visions as an inventor, but likely wasn't yet thinking of a technology that would make it possible to connect people across the globe in real time.

Nevertheless, it is simplicity that is appealing to people in a world where we often get overloaded with requests. It was the simplicity of people being able to post information and pictures about themselves to a large personal (or wider) community with a few clicks from almost anywhere that made social media a success on the Internet. It takes that same simplicity to motivate people to invest time to connect with others within their own organization.

Following is a list of those key success factors and lessons learned that you should be aware of, ordered by areas of applicability:

Building a Business Case

- Understand the motivations from those proposing to launch an ESN.

- Don't start a social media effort with the goal to run it as a top-management tool to inform your employees, rather create it with a genuine open mind of providing a conversation platform that belongs to all employees.
- Identify business areas that are split into silos and that could benefit from cross-communication and cross-learning.
- Get key stakeholders involved early and have them provide ongoing input into the requirements.
- If you explain your effort as "building an internal Facebook," make sure to point out some important differences between external social media platforms and ESNs.

Preparing the Organization

- Experiment with smaller scale social media initiatives to build some awareness and skills.
- Build some momentum around the new platform by explaining early on what will be coming.
- Involve the whole organization in choosing a name and building a brand—and do it early—ideally months before you actually launch anything.

Choosing a Good Solution

- The solution must be very simple to use. If you need to choose between feature-rich and simple, go for simple.
- Look at this as a long-term initiative not as a short-term project. Technology will only be one part of the solution.
- Don't spend all your money on the technology to the point that there is no funding left for supporting roles. Investments into initiative support will be the key for your ESN to become a success.
- When deciding whether to build something yourself or buy a solution off the shelf, take a close look at integration and extendibility needs, and at your in-house social media and web development skills.

Getting Started

- Get a pilot group involved—choose a diverse group coming from different regions as well as different functional areas.
- Open it up for feedback early—don't necessarily wait until it is all ready. Instead explain that it is still in progress and push it out to whoever wants it sooner rather than later.
- Don't be shy of internal marketing. Hit people with progress reports and information bits early and regularly.
- Make sure your key stakeholders understand that it is not a project with a defined start and end, but that it will need that ongoing support to survive and provide the anticipated business value.
- Get your most experienced social media experts (i.e., your bloggers) on board and get them to help you build momentum. Their feedback and experience will be priceless.

Roles

- Be aware of all the necessary roles that need to be played and identify candidates that can and will play them.
- Choose an open and passionate community manager that is likely to stick with the initiative longer-term.
- Keep your sponsors in the loop, show them progress, and get them passionate about the ESN.
- Make sure you have all the potential evangelizers identified and target them specifically. They will play the role of the first followers that help you create a movement.
- One person can play multiple roles, but ideally all of those multiple roles should be connected to the ESN and not to another business-critical task that is likely to take full priority over the ESN efforts.
- Don't forget your middle managers. They are role models, but often they issue concerns as to the immediate benefit of participating in social media activities and without having them in the boat, individuals might not feel comfortable to spend time on your ESN.

- Don't forget the role of the individual users. In the end they decide if your network will become a success or not.

Ongoing Success

- Get all stakeholders involved not only when launching it but have them involved on an ongoing basis as well.
- Rather than telling people to use your ESN, try to create a viral wave that will work via word-of-mouth and peer-recommendation.
- Train widely and often. Focus more on the business training than on the technical training. Shorter units like tips and tricks and short videos are more likely to reach the users.
- Go and meet your users where they are—for example, by running an info-booth in the cafeteria.
- Create some simple to digest but clear guidelines that will outline the borders and let people move freely within those borders. If you have people constantly pushing the boundaries find out why and adapt the guidelines if necessary.
- Create and manage a pulse, through regular and ongoing activities. It will give your initiative the lifeline it needs to survive longer-term.
- Executive buy-in is not enough—what you need is executive participation.

Technology

- Never forget that technology is only the enabler—it by itself will not make people contribute on an ongoing basis.
- Keep it simple. If you can make it easier for people to contribute, do it. If users ask for a lot of new features early on, push back if it will raise the complexity for the majority of users.
- Make sure people understand the conceptional power of such simple features like the little hashtag, which allows adding new dimensions across people and content within an ESN.

- Groups are not the same as communities of practice (CoP). It takes leadership, roles, and much more to have a CoP. ESN groups can be a good structural basis for creating a CoP around it, however.

Measuring

- Activity measurements can provide some information about where you are going, but they are limited in showing the real value. In order to measure value, focus on gaps that you want to close with your ESN and measure progress in closing them.
- Use social network analysis methods to visualize network connectivity. Make sure to also do a more detailed assessment on who the energizers and who the de-energizers in your network are.
- Employ more sophisticated social media analytics solutions that go beyond looking into the past to learn more about your user base and to make sure collaboration becomes a successful business process.
- Choose your KPIs (key performance indicators) carefully and check the validity of what they indicate repeatedly to make sure they actually drive the type of behavior that you had intended.
- Be careful with judging the value of certain absolute numbers. Look at progress as another way to get indications on how well your initiative is going.

Barriers

- Understand the main barriers as they apply to your organization.
- Work carefully with executive management on helping them to lose their fear of control by building a proper business case that contrasts the risks with the chances that an ESN offers.
- Make sure everyone understands the effects of destructive feedback and teach overcritical members of the organization the value of diversity.

- Reduce hurdles for entering the ESN world by offering application integration and capturing people where they are to guide them to the new way of collaborating.
- Be careful not to see the legal department as something that slows you down. Instead use them to help you create the type of frameworks that users can comfortably operate in so they don't have to take a guess with every post whether it might be legally compliant or not.

Appendix B Additional Resources

Barlow, Mike and David B. Thomas. *The Executive's Guide to Enterprise Social Media Strategy: How Social Networks Are Radically Transforming Your Business* (Wiley and SAS Business Series), 2011.

Blanchard, Olivier. *Social Media ROI, Managing and Measuring Social Media Efforts in Your Organization*, QUE Publishing, 2011.

Buckman, Robert. *Building a Knowledge-Driven Organization*, McGraw Hill, 2004.

Cross, Rob and Andrew Parker. *The Hidden Power of Social Networks, Understanding How Work Really Gets Done in Organizations*, Harvard Business Review Press, 2004.

Girard, John and Joanne Girard. *Leading Knowledge* — Under Creative Commons via http://itunes.apple.com/ch/book/leading-knowledge/id502118761?mt=11, accessed May 31, 2012.

Goleman, Daniel. *Social Intelligence, The New Science of Human Relationships*, Bantam, 2006.

Hagel III, John, John Seely Brown, and Lang Davison. *The Power of Pull: How Small Moves, Smartly Made, Can Set Big Things in Motion*, Basic Books, 2010.

Hubbard, Douglas W. *How to Measure Anything: Finding the Value of Intangibles in Business*, 2nd Edition, Wiley, 2010.

Leistner, Frank. *Mastering Organizational Knowledge Flow: How to Make Knowledge Sharing Work*, John Wiley & Sons, 2010.

Leonard, Dorothy and Walter Swap. *Deep Smarts, How to Cultivate and Transfer Enduring Business Wisdom*, Harvard Business School Press, 2005.

Li, Charlene and Josh Bernoff. *Groundswell Expanded and Revised Edition: Winning in a World Transformed by Social Technologies*, Harvard Business Press, 2011.

Penenberg, Adam L, *Viral Loop: From Facebook to Twitter, How Today's Smartest Business Grow Themselves*, Hyperion, 2009.

Prevou, Michael and Mitchell Levy. *#SUCCESSFUL CORPORATE LEARNING tweet Book05: Everything You Need to Know about Knowledge Management in Practice in 140 Characters or Less*, THiNKaha, 2012.

About the Author

Frank Leistner is Chief Knowledge Officer for SAS Global Professional Services. He has been in the IT industry for more than 20 years, beginning as a systems programmer for Nixdorf Computer in his home country of Germany and working from 1989 to 1993 for Siemens-Nixdorf in a liaison role out of Mountain View, California, focusing on the development of UNIX multi-processor operating systems. In 1993 Frank joined the European headquarters of SAS, shifting his focus to application development and field consulting. Based on his experiences in the field, he founded the SAS knowledge management program in 1997 and since then has been leading a range of knowledge exchange initiatives on a global level.

Between 1999 and 2003 Frank worked with the Institute for Knowledge Management led by IBM. In 2003 he was invited to the Harvard Graduate School of Education Learning Innovation Laboratory (LILA) roundtable. From 2005 on he worked with the Babson Working Knowledge Center, led by key KM pioneers Thomas Davenport and Laurence Prusak. He provided a chapter to *Leading with Knowledge: Knowledge Management Practices in Global Infotech Companies* (2003) and wrote case studies for a number of books published as part of knowledge management and business conferences. His book *Mastering Organizational Knowledge Flows: How to Make Knowledge Sharing Work* (Wiley, 2010) was well-received.

Frank holds an MSc in Computer Science from the State University of New York at Albany and a master's degree in Computer Science from the Technical University Carolo-Wilhelma in Braunschweig,

Germany. He has presented at numerous conferences and given keynotes in Europe and the United States about knowledge, talent management, Web 2.0, and social media topics.

You can visit his websites at http://masterknowledgeflow.ch and http://connectorgsilos.ch.

Index

(octothorpe), 4, 33, 127

A

Acronym tags, 129
Activity measures, 140–144
Adding a pulse, 91–93
Allen, Paul, 52
Altimeter Group (company), 140, 151
Amazon.com, 125
APIs (application programming interfaces), 121
Apple (company), 122
Archiving inactive groups, 133
Automation
  automated recommendations, 125–126
  power of simplicity in, 123–125
Avanade study, 55

B

Barriers to success
  dealing with "stupid" questions, 102–103
  fear of losing control, 97–100
  integration as, 103–110
  key success factors in, 179–180
  legal considerations, 111–114
  posting to multiple platforms, 110–111
  unlearning as, 100–101
Berger, Jonah, 84
Blogs and blogging
  about, 5
  author's, 173
  Booz-Allen, 96n
  The Hub case study, 45–46, 53–54
  mobilizing evangelizers, 74
Booz-Allen blog, 96n
Brokers, 154–155
Buckman, Bob, 140
Business case, building, 21, 140, 175–176

C

Case studies. *See* RedNet case study; The Hub case study
Channel overload, 162–163
Chatter tool, 51–52
CM (community manager) role
  about, 64–65, 76
  driving the pulse, 92
  managing groups, 131
Cognitive Edge (company), 29
Collaboration
  basis of, 145–146
  downsides of, 99
  innovation and, 168, 173
  interaction and, 168
  output of, 145
  as success driver, 145
  user funnel and, 40
  virtual teams and, 9

Communication
 analyzing, 143–147
 breaking isolation with, 26–29
 careful guidance for, 42
 corporate, 62–65, 76
 formal documentation as, 10
 HR department and, 71–72
 The Hub case study, 15, 39
 nonverbal, 26, 108
 notification management, 134–137
 openness in, 93–96
 RedNet case study, 15–16
 via ESNs, 48, 63, 68, 73
Communities of practice. *See* CoPs (communities of practice)
Community manager role. *See* CM (community manager) role
Community streams, 127
Company stream, 126
Confucius (philosopher), 61
Consumerization of IT, 55
Content
 contributing to social networks, 43
 role of emotions in distributing, 84
 technology considerations, 120
Control, fear of losing, 97–100
Coopetition, 167
CoPs (communities of practice)
 additional information, 17n
 community manager role and, 64
 critical mass for, 41
 defined, 9–10
 enabling innovation in, 34
 groups versus, 130–131
 mobilizing evangelizers, 74
 technology and, 130–134
 transferring knowledge in, 28–29
 virtual teams and, 9–10
Crowdsourcing, 42
Customers, ESNs and, 73–74, 76
Custom streams, 126–127

D

DaVinci, Leonardo, 175
Denning, Stephen, 29
Documentation
 as barrier to success, 103
 knowledge flow and, 6–7, 10
 storytelling and, 30
Dynamic organizations, handling, 32–33

E

Elias, Ric, 15
Email, social media shift from, 31–32, 101, 135–136
Emotions and content distribution, 84
ESNs (enterprise social networks)
 additional resources, 181
 breaking isolation with, 26–29
 as communication tools, 71–72
 defined, 2
 dynamics within, 24–26
 enabling innovation, 33–36
 enabling technology (*see* Technology)
 fighting barriers (*see* Barriers to success)
 getting started (*see* Launching ESNs)
 handling dynamic organizations, 32–33
 key success factors, 175–180
 laying the foundation for, 45–50
 motivations for introducing, 19–24
 organizational storytelling in, 29–32

partners and customers in, 73–74, 76
pre-conditions for getting started, 50–55
roles in, 9–10, 61–77
Evangelizer role, 66, 74–76, 83–84
Executive sponsor role, 63, 76
External social networks
contributing content to, 43
controlled environments and, 42
crowdsourcing and, 42
driving development in, 44
internal versus, 37–39
roles in, 62
scaling effectively, 43
size comparisons for, 39–41
training considerations, 42–43
user independence in, 41

F

Facebook social network
about, 39–40
connections in, 83
familiarity with, 116–117
Google+ and, 52
Instagram acquisition, 44–45
internal network equivalents, 118–120
Fear of losing control, 97–100
Fermi decomposition, 139–140
Find engines, 125–126
FISH! philosophy, 59n
Folksonomies, 10
Follower relationship, 149
Future Foundation study, 168

G

Gates, Bill, 139
Getting ESNs started. *See* Launching ESNs
Goodnight, Jim, 51
Google+, 52
Google facility tour, 55
Google search, 37–38, 115–116
Gretzky, Wayne, 79
Groups
archiving inactive, 133
communities versus, 130–131
creating, 132
in dynamic organizations, 33
as ESN roles, 66–74
leadership development, 71
managing, 131
mobilizing evangelizers, 74–76
pre-forming, 132
private, 33, 73, 103, 144, 153–154
technology, 66–68, 76, 120, 130–134
when launching ESNs, 47–48, 53–55
Group streams, 127
Groupthink, 99, 101
Guidelines, power of, 85–87

H

Hanseatic League, 26
Harvard Business Review, 22, 149
Hashtags
about, 4–5, 127–130
folksonomies and, 10
measuring value, 152–153
Home stream, 126
How to Measure Anything (Hubbard), 139
HR (human resources) department, 70–72, 76
Hubbard, Douglas W., 139, 144

The Hub case study
  about, 11–14
  breaking isolation in, 28–29
  communication examples, 92–93, 149
  external customer events and, 22
  handling dynamic organizations, 33
  integration in, 105–107
  interaction example, 8
  launching ESNs, 39, 45–54, 57
  mobilizing evangelizers, 74–75
  naming contest, 48–49
  network dynamics and, 25
  power of guidelines, 87
  roles in ESNs, 71
  social media analytics and, 144–146
  training sessions, 89
Humana (company), 92
Human resources (HR) department, 70–72, 76
Humor
  benefits of, 54
  cultural limitations of, 85

I

Independence of users in social networks, 41
Initiative launch approach, 55–56
Innovation
  collaboration and, 168, 173
  enabling, 33–36
  invention versus, 33–34
Instagram (company), 44–45
Integration
  as barrier to success, 103–110
  simplicity and, 123
  technology considerations, 121
  user satisfaction and, 67
Interaction
  costs of, 26
  creating value based on, 62
  The Hub case study, 8
  power of guidelines in, 87
  social network analysis on, 146–148
  storytelling in, 30
  as success driver, 145
  technology-assisted, 164
  trends in, 167–168
  virtual versus face-to-face, 9, 24
Internal social networks
  contributing content to, 43
  as controlled environments, 42
  crowdsourcing and, 42
  driving development in, 44
  external versus, 37–39
  mobilizing evangelizers in, 74–75
  scaling effectively, 43
  size comparisons for, 39–41
  training considerations, 42–43
  user independence in, 41
Invention versus innovation, 33–34
Isolation within organizations, 26–29

J

Jobs, Steve, 1, 19, 37, 115, 122
Jones, Lawrence H., 35

K

Kay, Alan, 157
Key performance indicators (KPIs), 151–155
KFM (knowledge flow management)
  barriers to (*see* Barriers to success)
  knowledge management comparison, xiv, 3–4
  launching ESNs, 46, 55–56

roles for, 76
social media versus, 10–11
trend toward, 7
KM (knowledge management)
combating knowledge loss, 28, 72, 148
knowledge flow management comparison, xiv, 3–4
KMI (knowledge flow initiative), 53, 91
Knowledge flow
documentation and, 6–7
social media and, xiv–xv, 7–11
Knowledge flow initiative (KMI), 53, 91
Knowledge loss, 28, 72, 148
KPIs (key performance indicators), 151–155

L

Launching ESNs
about, 55–56
adding a pulse, 91–93
executive buy-in, 93–96
going viral, 82–85
laying the foundation, 45–50
motivations for, 133
power of guidelines, 85–87
preconditions for getting started, 50–55
stakeholder involvement, 79–82
technology considerations, 56–58
training considerations, 87–90
Leadership development group, 71
Legal considerations
as barrier to success, 111–114
displaying employee pictures, 44
freedom within guidelines, 86–87
Legal department, 69–70, 76
Li, Charlene, 140, 144–145, 151–153
LinkedIn social network
about, 2–3
familiarity with, 116–117
Losing control, fear of, 97–100

M

MacDonald, Gagen, 27
Management roles
about, 69, 76
executive participation, 93–96
guiding internal initiatives, 42
Marketing
as ESN role, 63–64
internal versus external activities, 24
Mastering Organizational Knowledge Flow (Leistner), xiii, 4, 55, 61, 164
McKinsey study, 27
Measuring
performance indicators, 139–146
success factors, 179
Mentions stream, 126
Metadata, 4
Microblogging, 5–6. *See also* Twitter service
Microsoft Outlook, 135
Microsoft SharePoint, 57–58, 121
MIlkman, Katherine L., 84
Motivations
for achieving critical mass, 44–45
for introducing ESNs, 19–24, 133
for private groups, 154
Multidimensional navigation, 125–130

N

Navigation, multidimensional, 125–130
Networks and networking, 3. *See also* ESNs (enterprise social networks); Social media networks
New York Times, 84
Nielsen, Jakob, 50
NIH (not-invented-here) syndrome, 100
Nonverbal communication, 26, 108
Notification management, 134–137

O

Octothorpe (#), 4, 33, 127
On-boarding process, 27–28, 148
Organizational social media, 2
Organizational storytelling, 29–32
Ortho-Bionomy (product), 35

P

Partners, ESNs and, 73–74, 76
Pauls, Arthur Lincoln, 35–36
Posting-links, 146–147
Posts (blog), 5, 110–111
Pre-forming groups, 132
Private groups
  about, 103, 144
  examples of, 73
  The Hub case study, 33
  as measurement ratio, 153–154
Private streams, 126
Project launch approach, 55–56
Pulse, adding a, 91–93
Pyramid technology, 73

R

RedNet case study
  about, 15–17
  launching ESNs, 57
Red Ventures (company), 15–17
Reporting versus analytics, 146–151
Requirements-gathering phase, 80–82
Research and development department, 68
Retweeting messages, 83
Risk analysis, 99
Roles in ESNs
  individuals and departments, 68–74
  key success factors, 177
  mobilizing evangelizers, 74–76
  teams and communities, 74–76
  types of, 61–68
RSS feeds, 3

S

Saint-Exupéry, Antoine de, 97
SAS Institute, 11–14
Security considerations
  for technology, 120
  when launching ESNs, 111–112
Senge, Peter, 171
Siemens-Nixdorf (company), 73
Simplicity in technology, 120–125
Sivers, Derek, 74
SMA (social media analytics):
  about, 139–146
  choosing KPIs, 151–155
  reporting versus, 146–151
SNA (social network analysis), 141
Snowden, David, 29
Socialcast software platform, 48, 57–58
Social media analytics (SMA)
  about, 139–146
  choosing KPIs, 151–155
  reporting versus, 146–151

Social media networks. *See also* ESNs (enterprise social networks)
about, 1–2, 10–11
connection considerations, 2–3, 83
differences in, 39–45
internal versus external, 37–39
KFM versus, 10–11
knowledge flow and, xiv–xv, 7–11
organizational, 2
virtual teams and, 9
Social network analysis (SNA), 141
Sparks, Will, xiii
Sponsor role, 42, 63, 76
StackOverflow tool, 30–31
Storytelling, organizational, 29–32
Strategist role, 62–63
Streams (find tool), 126–127, 152
"Stupid" questions, 102–103
Success factors
about, 175
adding a pulse, 91–93
barriers to success, 179–180
building business cases, 175–176
choosing good solutions, 176
executive buy-in, 93–96
final thoughts, 171–173
getting started, 177
going viral, 82–85
measuring, 179
ongoing success, 178
power of guidelines, 85–87
preparing organizations, 176
roles, 177–178
stakeholder involvement, 79–82
technology, 178–179
training considerations, 87–90
Surowieki, James, 150
Syndication methods, 3

T

Tag-clouds, 5, 129
Tags
about, 4–5, 10, 127–130
acronym, 129
dynamic nature of, 33
measuring value of, 152–153
as metadata, 4
Teams
communities of practice and, 9–10
defined, 9–10
dynamic organizations and, 32
social media platforms and, 9
Technologist role, 66–68, 76
Technology
advances in, 157–162
balancing social interaction with, 164–166
determining user tools, 52
external versus internal social networks, 37–39
groups or communities, 66–68, 76, 120, 130–134
The Hub case study, 48
internal Facebook equivalents, 118–120
key success factors for, 178–179
launching ESNs, 56–58
multidimensional navigation, 125–130
notification management, 134–137
power of simplicity in, 120–125
scaling social networks, 43
tools supporting, 115–118
TED videos, 74
ToolPool initiative, 36
Topic clusters, analyzing, 147
Training considerations, 42–43, 87–90

Trend lists and graphs, 129
Twitter service
  about, 4–6
  connections in, 83
  familiarity with, 116
  hashtags in, 4–5, 10, 127–130, 152–153

U

Unlearning prior knowledge, 100–101
URL shorteners, 6
User funnel, 40
User independence in social networks, 41
User role, 66, 76

V

Value indicators, 144–145
Viral spread, 82–85
Virtual teams. *See* Teams
VMware Socialcast, 48, 57–58

W

Water cooler analogy, 29–32
Weblogs. *See* Blogs and blogging
Wenger, Etienne, 17n
The Wisdom of Crowds (Surowieki), 150

X

Xing platform, 116–117